Research Series on the Chinese Dream and China's Development Path

Drawing on a large body of empirical studies done over the last two decades, the *Research Series on the Chinese Dream and China's Development Path* seeks to provide its readers with in-depth analyses of the past and present, and forecasts for the future course of China's development. Thanks to the adoption of Socialism with Chinese characteristics, and the implementation of comprehensive reform and opening, China has made tremendous achievements in areas such as political reform, economic development, and social construction, and is making great strides towards the realization of the Chinese dream of national rejuvenation. In addition to presenting a detailed account of many of these achievements, the authors also discuss what lessons other countries can learn from China's experience. This series will be an invaluable companion to every researcher who is trying to gain a deeper understanding of the development model, path and experience unique to China.

More information about this series at http://www.springer.com/series/13571

Yiming Yuan
Editor

Studies on China's Special Economic Zones

SSAP

Springer

Editor
Yiming Yuan
China Center for Special Economic
Zone Research
Shenzhen University
Shenzhen, Guangdong
China

ISSN 2363-6866 ISSN 2363-6874 (electronic)
Research Series on the Chinese Dream and China's Development Path
ISBN 978-981-10-3703-0 ISBN 978-981-10-3704-7 (eBook)
DOI 10.1007/978-981-10-3704-7

Jointly published with Social Sciences Academic Press

Library of Congress Control Number: 2016963745

Printed on acid-free paper

This Springer imprint is published by Springer Nature
The registered company is Springer Nature Singapore Pte Ltd.
The registered company address is: 152 Beach Road, #21-01/04 Gateway East, Singapore 189721, Singapore

Preface

Studies on China's Special Economic Zones was inaugurated in 2008 at the China Center for Chinese Special Economic Zone Research, Shenzhen University, a Ministry of Education-designated key humanities and social sciences research base. Professor Yuan Yiming of the Center was the founding chief editor of the journal, a yearly publication. After eight editions, *Studies on China's Special Economic Zones* is now available in full text in the Chinese National Knowledge Infrastructure (CNKI) database, a testament to its excellence as an academic serial publication.

The establishment of Special Economic Zones (SEZ) is now recognized as a worldwide phenomenon that plays a significant role in the process of economic takeoff and development. Many developing countries are seeking to adopt the development path that features SEZ as a part of its core strategy, and China has much to share with them about its successful experiences with SEZ development. At this journal, we are committed to bringing our readers the latest research findings on both theoretical and practical SEZ-related issues, in Shenzhen and beyond. We also publish studies of other countries' experience in this area and what China's own SEZ development path means for the rest of the world. We want the journal to become a premium platform for international exchange on this important topic. *Studies on China's Special Economic Zones* is the only academic journal in China devoted entirely to SEZ studies and is international in its editorial orientation.

The journal features articles written by a stellar group of academics, researchers, and scholars from prestigious organizations and institutions both inside and outside China. So far, the roster has included Justin Yifu Lin, the former World Bank Chief Economist, who contributed two long research articles during his tenure in that post; Hailemeskel Tefera, secretary of State of Ethiopia; and Marilou Uy, the sector director for the Africa Financial and Private Sector Development Department at the World Bank, among others.

A bilingual publication printed in both Chinese and English *Studies on China's Special Economic Zones* has been well received not only by international institutions such as the World Bank and the African Development Bank but also government officials as well as scholars from 13 emerging economies, including

Vietnam, Pakistan, South Korea, Cambodia, India, Rwanda, and Ethiopia. As its influence continues to grow, the journal has become an important source of reference for foreign researchers and policy-makers alike trying to draw from China's experience with developing SEZs, such as represented by Shenzhen, while building their own Special Economic Zones. The World Bank, Korea Development Institute, African Development Bank, and Peking University are just some of the institutions that now subscribe and carry the journal, which has also drawn raving reviews from high-ranking government officials in more than 20 countries in Africa. *Studies on China's Special Economic Zones*'s status as a cutting-edge serial publication in SEZ studies with sold citation track record is well established. We hope the journal will continue to grow robustly in the years ahead.

Shenzhen, China Yiming Yuan

Contents

Sponsor

Key Research Base for Humanities and Social Sciences of Ministry of Education, P.R.C
China Center for Special Economic Zone Research, Shenzhen University
Editor-in-chief: Yiming Yuan
Assistant Editor-in-Chief: Yikun Zhou

Special Economic Zones and China's Path

Tao Yitao

Abstract China's path lies in setting up special economic zones to accomplish the transformation of the system and in establishing a market economic system to seek a road of development from widespread poverty to prosperity for all. The establishment of special economic zones opened the road to scientific development in Chinese society and presented a shortcut for Chinese society to achieve modernization amidst extreme disequilibrium of development among regions, between urban areas and rural areas. The practice of tortuous reforms and the opening up accompanied by remarkable achievements in China's special economic zones, represented by Shenzhen, reveals the distinctiveness of China's characteristic path for realizing modernization and offers a choice of developmental path to be adopted by transitional countries and emerging countries with a market economy.

Keywords Special economic zones · Institutional change · China's path · Shenzhen

As the outcome of special policies, a special economic zone is an epoch-making hallmark of rationality and fever, thinking and blindness in the modern history of China. It marks the beginning of Chinese society's transformation from a planned economy to a market economy and also the real opening up of China's gateway that had been closed for 30 years. It is a sign of an ideological emancipation and a renewal of a way of thinking. It indicates that a large country on the verge of economic collapse can really embark on a path towards scientific development. Therefore, in view of the social and political background at the beginning of the reform and opening up, a special economic zone is certainly the only road for Chinese society to embark on in order to transform itself from a planned economy to a market economy so as to initiate social transformation in an all-round way; from the perspective of exploration regarding the road towards modernization, a special economic zone undoubtedly serves as the inevitable path for thoroughly breaking away from the conflicts between the ideal and reality in order to take the

T. Yitao (✉)
China Center for Special Economic Zone Research, Shenzhen University, Shenzhe, China

Y. Yuan (ed.), *Studies on China's Special Economic Zones*, Research Series on the Chinese Dream and China's Development Path,
DOI 10.1007/978-981-10-3704-7_1

socialist road with Chinese characteristics to arrive at prosperity for all; in terms of choosing the path for China's institutional change, a special economic zone is unquestionably the only way to break out of the rigid conventional system and the doctrine of ideology so as to complete the institutional change of a transitional society from top to bottom in a traditional socialist country once dominated by traditional ideology; with regard to a developmental strategy, a special economic zone is indisputably the only road for a country once overwhelmed by ultra-left ideology to embark on in order to truly abandon the blind developmental concepts that "man can conquer nature" and "development is fostered only for the sake of development", and thus pursue scientific development.

I. **The institutional change of Chinese society, mainly highlighted by the establishment of the market economic system, constitutes a glorious course in the growth and development of the special economic zones. The practice of the reform and opening up full of twists and turns but giving birth to outstanding achievements in China's special economic zones, represented by the Shenzhen Special Economic Zone, not only reveals the uniqueness, main features and future developmental trends of China's characteristic path for achieving modernization, but also provides a choice of path to be adopted by transitional countries and emerging market economy countries on the basis of its correct choice of path and fabulous development.**

"China's path" mentioned here means that special economic zones are set up in China to complete the transformation of the system, and the market economic system is established to enable all-round social and economic development in China. More precisely, in a large country that has had a planned economy for 30 years and where traditional ideology undoubtedly prevails, special economic zones have been established to make a breakthrough in institutional change designed to break the traditional system, with a view to gradually transforming from the planned economy to a market economy nationwide and to seeking a path from widespread poverty to prosperity for all, so that the market economy can be established in Chinese society in a short time and really turn China into an economically prosperous, institutionally developed, country that is based on laws and that has a socialist market economy.

China's road to modernization not only attracts the widespread attention of scholars, but it is also the ideal to which several generations of politicians and personages of noble aspirations have dedicated their lifetime. We once sincerely, hopelessly "learnt from the advanced technologies and experience of foreigners with the aim of doing better than them"; we even had the fever of trying to unrealistically and awkwardly "surpass Great Britain and catch up with the United States"; however, the road to reaching goals runs counter to those goals, thus the Chinese who were afraid of being poor had to reflect on the correctness of the chosen road. After drawing comparisons regarding the characteristics of modernization in major countries in the 19th century and the 20th century, some scholars pointed out that the capitalist road to modernization in the 19th century combined private property rights with market competition and it formed naturally after hundreds of years. Private ownership, market orientation and gradual change are the basic characteristics of this mode. In the 20th century, some backward countries took the socialist road, got involved in a top-down compulsory industrialization process guided by aggressive political revolution, with an attempt to rapidly achieve modernization via the Soviet mode with a national plan and radical reform on the basis of pure public ownership. Such a mode met with a crisis after a brief success [1]. Scholars widely believed that China did not really embark on the road to modernization which was proved to be correct by practice until 1990s. This is a road to socialist modernization with Chinese characteristics—the establishment of special economic zones aimed at the reform and opening up planned by Deng Xiaoping [2].

Historically, the reform and opening up initiated 35 years ago started from building an oasis of the market economy amid the vast sea of the planned economy in China. As a place with the weakest planned economy in China at that time, Shenzhen was the first to become an oasis thanks to its geographical advantages (proximity to Hong Kong, Macau, remoteness from the center of the planned economy). When Comrade Deng Xiaoing, the chief architect of China's reform and opening up, thinker and initiator of China's institutional change, returned to power for the third time, the severest challenge and test for him was how to achieve modernization across the board in a large country on the brink of social and economic collapse. The blind and crazy socialist practice for nearly half a century and the situation of China's socioeconomic development at that time had clearly proved that the planned economy was unfeasible, nor were the strategies for blindly catching up with and surpassing other countries and the equalitarianism of a small-scale peasant economy feasible. In a large backward country which was sustained by the equalitarianism of the planned economy and saw widespread poverty, the only way to shake off poverty consisted in breaking the institutional mechanism leading to widespread poverty within the system and taking a non-balanced developmental road. Such a road towards development is what was advocated by Deng Xiaoping—allowing part of the people and regions to get well-off first.

As a compulsory institutional arrangement, the establishment of special economic zones broke the general state of equilibrium resulting in widespread poverty in the traditional system, so that the social change characterized by non-balanced development became the best road towards the institutional change in Chinese society, and China, a large country governed by a planned economy for half a century, was able to move in a short time from the "plan" as a cause for widespread poverty to the "market" allowing part of the people to become prosperous first. As a formal top-down institutional arrangement, the establishment of special economic zones has not only greatly reduced the resistance to institutional change, cut down the costs for institutional innovations, but it has also successfully prevented reform from possibly bringing about more risks, thus it is possible for performance in institutional change to quickly emerge and fruitfully play an exemplary role nationwide within a short period of time.

China's path should be a road towards modernization with Chinese characteristics. "Chinese characteristics" are defined at country-specific, national, historical and international levels rather than deny the essential connotation of modernization and the inherent value judgment. Therefore, "Chinese characteristics" only lie in the distinctiveness of the road towards achieving goals and the choice of that road for reaching goals instead of the goals themselves. "Chinese characteristics" involve the process by which human beings recognize universal values, and they are anything but a disavowal of international conventions. As a choice of a road down which one nation, rather than a city, marches towards modernization, China's special economic zones, represented by the Shenzhen Special Economic Zone, are written in the annals of China's reform and opening up and will also go down in the history of changes in the world's economic pattern.

II. **In a broader sense, especially in terms of a traditional system and a developmental model in the period of planned economy, establishing special economic zones was the critical choice for scientific development, and it opened up the road to scientific development in Chinese society. The growth and development of China's special economic zones, represented by the Shenzhen Special Economic Zone, entails exactly the process of continuously adjusting its developmental strategy amidst lessons and setbacks, optimizing the industrial structure, transforming the developmental model and exploring a gradual shift from a society driven by economic growth to a welfare-oriented society with full-fledged development. The philosophy of scientific development has expanded the "outlook on development" from the transformation of the growth pattern to social development and from the economic field to various fields of social life. As the most successful special economic zone in China, Shenzhen gives expression to China's path and its connotations through the course of its own development.**

The transformation from a planned economy to a market economy is none other than the transformation of Chinese society from the strategy of catching up with and overtaking other countries to the strategy for non-balanced development. Compared with the "blind development outlook" in the period of planned economy, establishing special economic zones doubtlessly carved out a correct path towards scientific development of Chinese society. People in some areas have a one-sided understanding of the correct judgment that "development is of overriding importance"; moreover, they have a "lopsided outlook on development" that regards pursuing development at the expense of the environment and of the citizens' welfare, while the outlook on scientific development certainly charts a path towards development for sustainable growth. The outlook on scientific development negates the ultra-left thought that "man can conquer nature" and thoroughly rectifies the blind developmental outlook that "development must be pursued at all costs"; more importantly, it establishes the slogan that "development is of overriding importance"—a correct developmental philosophy which reflects the important motive power and objective for human survival and life. The essence of the outlook on scientific development is development rather than reluctance to develop. The outlook on scientific development is by no means directed against the correct judgment that "development is of overriding importance"; instead, it emphasizes the scientificity and correctness of the social developmental model, method, pattern and choice of path to achieve it. It is anything but a debate on whether development should be fostered or not. It is firmly believed that only when the philosophy of scientific development is established can China's special economic zones come into being, and can hundreds of millions of people have the pursuit of common prosperity and China's economy can be brilliant for 35 years.

The development of the Shenzhen Special Economic Zone is a process in which the developmental strategy was continuously adjusted amid lessons and setbacks, the industrial structure was optimized, and the economic development model was transformed; moreover, there was also investigation into a gradual shift from a society driven by economic growth to a welfare-oriented society with all-round development. The development of the Shenzhen Special Economic Zone started from processing materials supplied by foreign clients, processing according to buyer's samples, assembling parts supplied by foreign clients and engaging in compensation trade. The selection of such a developmental model was determined by factor endowment available at that time. Shenzhen was just a little-known small fishing village less subject to a planned economic system at the initial stage of the reform and opening up. Comparatively advantageous production factors in Shenzhen at that time were cheap labor force and land, while Shenzhen fell short in capital, technologies and management. This coincided with the industrial upgrading and structural adjustment of Hong Kong's economy, thus guided by the policy of reform and opening-up, labor-intensive industries dominated by the processing industry which timely and appropriately established itself in Shenzhen where the manufacturing industry was urgently needed, while industrial transfer was accompanied by a gradual shift of capital, technologies, management and the modern enterprise system to the growing Shenzhen. With efforts to carry forward a chain of industrial renewal from territories and countries with a developed market economy, Shenzhen not only reduced the costs for jumpstarting economic development, but it also greatly lowered the costs for learning from a market economy, determining the basic characteristic which defines an outward-looking economy. Meanwhile, the "importation" of processing and manufacturing industries also gave rise to derivative demand, thus stimulating the rise and development of the tertiary industry. As of 1993, 87% of Shenzhen's foreign trade came from the net export from Chinese-foreign joint ventures, Chinese-foreign cooperative enterprises and wholly foreign-owned enterprises and the income from processing materials supplied by foreign clients, processing according to buyer's samples, assembly parts supplied by foreign clients and from engaging in compensation trade; the tertiary industry accounted for 46% of Shenzhen's GDP and labor force absorbed by the tertiary industry made up 32.2% of the employed people in Shenzhen [3].

As Shenzhen embarked on the track of rapid economic growth, the constraints from the inherent shortage of natural resources in Shenzhen emerged soon and aroused the concern of policymakers. Such a shortage means that under the law of scarcity, with any choice of a growth pattern based on consumption and use of natural resource factors, people have to pay a relatively high price for wealth creation and development so that the price for economic growth will also increase with the high costs of the creation of wealth. Meanwhile, as an emerging city which became the first to practice the market economy, Shenzhen could not repeat the developmental model and path of traditional industry and was more willing to explore and try out a novel economic growth mode and wealth creation route, thus setting a good example nationwide.

With a shift from focusing on processing materials supplied by foreign clients, processing according to buyer's samples, assembling parts supplied by foreign clients and engaging in compensation trade to develop new high-tech industries as a backbone, Shenzhen chose a path for sustainable development in due time. The leading force of government decision-making in institutional change (the establishment of special funds and the adoption of preferential policies, etc.) addressed financing the gap resulting from high input at the early stage and relieved the pressure on new high-tech enterprises for taking risks alone. With the broad mind peculiar to reformers, actions have been taken to foster the institutional environment for new high-tech enterprises to settle, grow, develop and innovate in Shenzhen and attract a large number of well-known domestic and foreign new high-tech enterprises to Shenzhen. With the foresight and sagacity of innovators, a solid intellectual guarantee has been provided for the subsequent development of new high-tech industries and some well-known universities and a variety of scientific research institutions have taken root in Shenzhen. By 2000, the output of computer magnetic heads in Shenzhen ranked No. 3 in the world, the output of microelectronic computers, stored program control exchanges and genetic interferon accounted for 25, 50 and 60% of the total national output respectively, and Shenzhen was also the largest production base for printers, hard disk drives and cordless telephones nationwide; moreover, five large new high-tech pillar industries, including electronic information, biotechnology, new materials, optical, mechanical and electronic integration and lasers, had taken shape [3].

Imitation was the main way for increasing the output value of new and high technologies in China for a considerably long time. However, the real international competitiveness of a country cannot be derived from a shortcut and instant benefits brought about by imitation for a long time. The creativity of industries, namely the original innovation capability, the integrated innovation capability and the capability for introduction, assimilation, absorption and re-innovation, are the fundamental sources for the permanent vitality of an enterprise and the lasting competitiveness of a country. Therefore, self-dependent innovation has been put forward as a strategic way of thinking, giving full expression to the philosophy of sustainable development.

Theoretically, self-dependent innovation is a kind of innovation activity that is higher than imitation. It builds a new production function or incorporates an unprecedented "new combination" of production factor and production system into the production process. It stresses the applications of inventions in economic activities and delivers profits to parties involved in production. Therefore, self-dependent innovation emphasizes self-research and development, ownership of core technologies, and it underscores the added value of technologies and patents in the process of value creation. In this sense, self-dependent innovation is the inevitable requirement for transformation of the economic growth mode and also an important way to achieving such transformation. This is because whether self-dependent innovation features "neutral technical progress" (unchanged proportion of factor input), "labor-saving technical progress" or "capital-saving technical progress", it increases output on the premise of neither increasing nor decreasing the use of factors to improve the efficiency of resource utilization. This means that we cannot be merely content with the simple "imitation" of advanced foreign technologies and cannot just rest on the mode of the introduction of extensive, low-level technology dominated by the importation of equipment at the early stage of the reform and opening up; instead, we need to rethink and determine the economic growth mode by which to export "soft technologies" and increase the contribution from self-dependent innovation (creation of core technologies) to GDP.

The labor-intensive processing and manufacturing industry based on processing materials supplied by foreign clients, processing according to buyer's samples, assembling parts supplied by foreign clients and engaging in compensation trade has formed, and the capital, technology-intensive high and new technology industry has developed; and the philosophy of self-dependent innovation has taken shape in the economic field so as to bring about social and economic development through the transformation of the economic growth mode, while the philosophy of scientific development has expanded the "developmental outlook" from the transformation of the growth mode to social development and from the economic field to various fields of social life. Solving and correcting developmental problems by the cognition of scientific development and the philosophy of harmonious development after the achievement of brilliant successes and accumulation of wealth represents the deep-rooted reflections and way of thinking regarding moving the city of Shenzhen forward.

Today, Shenzhen, established 30 years ago, has entered a mature period of steady growth. Over the years, Shenzhen's economy has grown at a rate of over 15%, and its economic aggregate skyrocketed from 196 million yuan at the beginning of its establishment to 820,123 million yuan in 2009, and per-capita GDP soared from 606 yuan in 1979 to 93,000 yuan in 2009.[1] In a sense, Shenzhen has followed a track of rapid growth to bring wealth and prosperity to the struggling people. As we know, GDP is the material base for social development, but it is by no means the ultimate goal for social development. GDP and per-capita GDP growth not accompanied by an improvement in social welfare is nothing but pure material growth without a soul and humanistic care.

[1]Data on GDP and per-capita GDP during the period 1979–2008 come from the *Shenzhen Statistical Yearbook (2008)*, while those concerning GDP and per-capita GDP in 2009 come from Shenzhen Statistics Online. http://www.sztj.com/pub/sztjpublic/tjsj/tjyb/default.html.

The labor-intensive economy has allowed Shenzhen to build competitive power with a price advantage in seizing the market as a result of low costs, while the global financial crisis has further laid bare the problems stemming from the economic growth mode and concerning low added value of capital and technologies, lack of competitive power in the labor-intensive economy, and it has also seriously presented the transformation of an economic developmental model as the inevitable strategic choice for scientific development.

Comparative advantage is an important principle for seeking economic development in different countries and territories. Such an advantage is a comparative advantage of factor price determined by the degree of the relative scarcity of factors. When labor resources are relatively abundant and thus labor costs or prices are relatively low in a country or territory, with the absence of capital and the advantages of the technological factor endowment, first utilizing the cheap labor peculiar to it has become the best natural choice with the lowest developmental cost in the period of economic take-off. Comparative advantage of the latter was exactly the main choice for the economic take-off and initial development in Shenzhen, even for that in the whole country at the early stage of the reform and opening up.

Scarcity is the basic premise and general principle for economics. Economics research touches upon how a society makes use of scarce resources to produce valuable goods and services, and distributes them among different people. However, most of the economically backward developing countries are subject to resource constraints in the sense of factor structure rather than lack of resources in terms of natural endowment. Resource constraints in the sense of factor structure means that factor endowment structure is at a low level, in other words, there is a lack of relatively high-level factors such as capital, technology, education, management and legal system but a crop of uneducated or less educated ordinary labor is available in the economic development of a country or territory. Therefore, the root cause for low economic structure lies in the low factor endowment structure instead of structure itself. If there is only simple labor in the stock of factors in a country, the labor-intensive economy is a natural choice. The economic structure cannot be artificially changed merely by wish in any economy because changing the quality and structure of factors is the practical, logical precondition for improving the industrial structure [4]. Nietzsche said, “Nothing is scarcer than sane honesty in a philosopher” [5]. The advance of human society needs not only diligence and passion but also thinking and rationality.

III. **When the economic value of people is increased, our society will be in some new and better fields of opportunity. The government should not lead the social economy with its own wishful thinking; instead, it must create an institutional environment to finish the supply of public goods and foster a social welfare mechanism while respecting the market. Development is the result of reform and also the material prerequisite for intensifying reform, but development cannot replace reform. If there is no reform of the political system suitable to the economic system, the reform of the economic system cannot become truly successful. On the**

unique "Chinese path" towards modernization in the course of building a civil society based on laws, as the areas given the first priority for development, China's special economic zones should show a sign of hope for tomorrow—further promoting reform through the opening up and proceeding first with implementation and experimentation to boost the intensification of reforms in Chinese society so as to make the society civilized, prosperous and strong through a reform of the government.

Schurz believed, "the impact from long-term change of any economy on institutional change is more far-reaching than that from change in wages on rent" [6]. "The improvement in the economic value of people spurs new needs for systems, while some political and legal systems are designed to meet those needs" [6]. Human capital calls for making clear the situation of the social system in the case of seeking its own right to participation, thus many systems are created as a result of incentives for economic growth; for example, in a mature market economy, the people's need for convenience with respect to currency has shifted to the need for rights; as economic growth increasingly depends upon the progress of knowledge, people will shift their need for the systems capable of generating and distributing this knowledge to the need for its rights; as the people's living standard increases, everyone will switch from the need for an additional guarantee against accidents to the need for rights, as well as the need for health and life insurance; with social progress, the need of people for a legal guarantee attached to personal rights (such as protection against police violations, loss of personal privacy) will also turn to the need for rights such as the people's need for civic rights; as a factor in production, people need more equality in getting jobs, especially hi-tech jobs, and people hope to encounter less discrimination in getting hi-tech jobs through on-the-job training and higher education [6].

As human capital is non-material, its survival and growth needs an institutional environment for maintenance. It creates wealth for the society and presents the society with the institutional requirements for its guarantee. It boosts the growth of the social economy while increasing its own economic value. The increase—originating from economic development and institutional performance—in the economic value of people motivates the formation of a social institutional environment more beneficial for the survival of human capital. A good social institutional environment is conducive to the formation and re-creation of human capital and also helps increase the rate of return on human capital investment. Meanwhile, the institutional change corresponding to the increase in the economic value of people calls for a new economic model and growth mode. In this sense, the real power leading to the transformation of an economic developmental model does not lie in subjective wishes, but comes from the improvement in the economic value of people which constitutes an internal mechanism and motivation in the economic society.

In his book *Development as Freedom*, Amartya Sen states that development can be taken as a process of expanding the real freedom which people enjoy. The developmental outlook which focuses on human freedom is in striking contrast with a narrower developmental outlook. A narrow developmental outlook covers the views that development equals an increase in GDP or a boost in personal income, or industrialization, or technical progress, or social modernization, etc.... However, freedom also hinges on other decisive factors such as economic arrangements in a society (such as education and healthcare facilities), political and civic rights (such as the freedom for developing views in public discussion)... Development requires the elimination of the main factors which restrict people's freedom, namely, poverty and tyranny, a lack of economic opportunity, systematic social deprivation, ignorance of public facilities, intolerance and excessive intervention from a repressive regime. With the conscience, morals and wisdom of a scholar, Amartya Sen answers the question regarding the goal for the development of human society: as it is people-centered, the highest goal and value standard for social development is freedom. Wealth, income, technical progress, social modernization, etc. are the goals pursued by people, but they ultimately fall within the scope of tools and serve the development and welfare of the people.

China's social reform unfolds at a relatively low per-capita income level since, on the one hand, a huge middle class has not yet taken shape; on the other hand, the gap between the rich and the poor has become increasingly salient and wide. Therefore, poverty amid economic growth and low welfare in economic prosperity have "prematurely" become the social problems which the government must solve through institutional arrangement. Affirmatively, the government must treat the establishment of a social welfare system as the guarantee for achieving common prosperity, rather than as the result of common prosperity. In any society, the creation of wealth begets poverty and the achievement of prosperity is followed by decreasing happiness in part of the people, which is more dreadful than widespread poverty. A welfare system, a system which is not an article of luxury for economic development, makes up the important contents of development and becomes an integral part of substantive freedom. Actually, when it comes to the slogan, put forward at the beginning of reform, that we must emancipate the productive forces, and the philosophy of development, advocated today, that we must put people first and build a harmonious society, their essential connotation consists of emancipating the people and empowering the subject of social economy—the people—with a feasible capacity for enjoying such life which there is a reason to cherish. People can obtain rights while creating wealth, secure respect while increasing wealth, share social surplus while contributing to the society, and experience human dignity in a normal social mechanism.

There is an inherent correlation between the market and the basic freedom of people. It is not impartial that people praise the market mechanism merely from the perspective of efficiency. Market failure may become the important basis for people to deny the market, yet market failure does not negate but suggests perseverance in the market mechanism—the market should do what it can do, while the government should do what the market fails to do and what the market can't do well. Government power plays an indispensable role in compulsory institutional change characterized by top-down authorization. However, subject to the law of the market, any overwhelming governmental power does not duly correct market failure but destroys the law of the market. The government should refrain from leading the social economy with its own wishes and create an institutional environment, supply public goods and develop a social welfare mechanism while respecting the market.

The reform of Chinese society started in the economic field, which, undoubtedly, was the best way, but quickly brought to light such problems as the absence of supporting resources in the general social environment and a lack of effective institutional environment, and led to system and institutional bottlenecks in intensifying reform. Systems are embedded within an institutional environment. Institutional change cannot be really accomplished without an institutional environment. Likewise, if a reform of the political system fit for a reform of the economic system is unavailable, the reform of the economic system cannot become truly successful. Fundamentally, many problems and contradictions at the present time were a result of a lag in the reform of the political system.

In a transforming society, the establishment of a brand-new social operating mechanism entails the process in which the powers and vested interests of government officials are crippled, deprived, and even lost, and a service-oriented government forms, develops and grows. In a system within which government powers must be deprived in themselves, the level of civilization and the foresight of the government are crucial for the institutional performance of a society.

Our society will not perish just because there is a lack of miracles; however, its vitality will not endure if the thinking which creates miracles is not available. As the special marks of miracles and miracle-creating thinking, special economic zones not only inject infinite vitality into Chinese society but they also bring limitless hope for this nation to create miracles.

References

1. Luo Rongqu: Retrospect of the 20th Century and Prospect for the 21st Century —— From the Perspective of the Process of the World's Modernization (J), *Strategy & Management*, 1996(3).
2. Zhang Yanguo: Comparative Research and Analysis of the Modernization Thoughts of Mao Zedong and Deng Xiaoping (J), *Wuhan University Journal* (Philosophy & Social Sciences), 2004(3).
3. Tao Yitao, Lu Zhiguo ed.: *Theory on the History of China's Special Economic Zones* (M), Social Sciences Academic Press, 2008.
4. Fan Gang: Theories & Practice in the Past and in the Future (J), quoted from Yuan Yiming ed.: *Studies on China's Special Economic Zones* (M), Social Sciences Academic Press, 2009.
5. Fredrich Nietzsche: *Will to Power: Attempt at a Revaluation of All Values* (M), The Commercial Press, 1991.
6. T·W Schurz: Continuous Improvement in the Economic Value of Institution and People (J), *American Journal of Agricultural Economics*, 1968(50).

The Dynamic Evolution of China's Special Economic Zones and Their Practice

Yuan Yiming

Abstract The establishment of special economic zones is a crucial strategic choice for China's development, and developing special economic zones first in order to stimulate the economic take-off of the whole country is China's way towards modernization, which is exerting a profound and far-reaching impact all around the world. In practice, China's special economic zones have dynamically evolved in terms of time dimension, in 35 years, by shifting a focus from institutional experiment to regional development to developmental issues, and changing the desired function from "overall" to "strategically regional" to "specifically local", with its essential connotation characterized by institutional experiment—comprehensive practice—path exploration; however, in general, the historical procedure of China's special economic zones centers on a target system, a developmental path and an institutional change mode for finding answers.

Keywords Special economic zones · Dynamic evolution · Choice of path

Special economic zones represent the choice of a path for avoiding risks on the route towards China's institutional reform, and they are basically designed to become the optimal combination of risks and institutional change, thus China's special economic zones are certainly of an institutional experimental nature during transformation from the planning system to a market economic system and are defined as experimental zones for reform.

In terms of the routine process, the dynamic evolution of China's special economic zones in 35 years resulted from a correct and incisive assessment of the situation by policymakers of the State. A systematic analysis shows that there is a dynamically deepening endogenous mechanism—a supply and demand mechanism for the institutional arrangement of special economic zones. Serious failure of the planning system occurred 35 years ago, leading to a severe lack of an efficient

---

Y. Yiming (✉)
China Center for Special Economic Zone Research, Shenzhen University, Shenzhen, China

Y. Yuan (ed.), *Studies on China's Special Economic Zones*, Research Series on the Chinese Dream and China's Development Path,
DOI 10.1007/978-981-10-3704-7_2

economic system in China. Subsequently, special zones, including Shenzhen and Zhuhai, came into being. In the 1990s, spatial growth poles were increasingly important and severely inadequate; as a result, Shanghai and Tianjin became the important choices as the second-generation special zones. Developmental contradictions cropped up and specific regions were underdeveloped in the new period, thus the third-generation special economic zones emerged. Policymakers were wise to address the internal institutional needs in China's economic development, and they were courageous to remove ideological and thought dissensions, making such an endogenous mechanism a reality. In my opinion, the establishment and operation of such an endogenous mechanism is the important contents of China's path and also the primary cause for the difference between China's special economic zones and general special economic zones around the world.

1 The Dynamic Evolution of the Special Zones: From Institution-Focused Special Zones to Path-Focused Special Zones

The special economic zone phenomenon of great significance was formed on China's distinctive economic take-off and developmental path built in more than 30 years. Special economic zones established and developed during China's modernization are essentially different from the existing special economic zones around the world, while this difference originates from the differences in the starting point for establishing special zones (China's starting point is the planning system), basic motive for their establishment (the fundamental purpose for their establishment in China is to explore the economic system and developmental path) and connotation (though the construction of China's special economic zones focuses on the economic field, it also covers the administrative system, cultural reform, social construction, etc.).

The above differences determine the fact that the development of China's special economic zones features first, implementation in terms of time and experiment with regard to function (the experimental zone of the economic system), thus China's special economic zones have the nature of an institutional experiment and there is the Chinese-style development of the special economic zones compared with international special zones with a single function (introduction of foreign capital or export processing).

China's special economic zones are made up of special economic zones, new development and opening-up zones, free trade zones, etc. in different periods. In view of the logical basis for establishment, function and connotation, three generations of special economic zones arose and rapidly evolved in China in more than 30 years.

The first-generation special economic zones, represented by Shenzhen: four special economic zones concurrently established in the 1980s—Shenzhen, Zhuhai,

Shantou and Xiamen—share a common spatial feature—almost each special economic zone engaged in specific, well-targeted cooperation: Shenzhen is adjacent to Hong Kong, and Zhuhai is close to Macau, while Xiamen is opposite Taiwan, only Shantou has a broad and vague geographic space for cooperation since its cooperation involves overseas regions where there are a great number of immigrants from the Chaozhou-Shantou region.

It is evident that the first-generation special economic zones are based on strictly consistent logic for selection due to geographical location, while precise selection of the geographical location ensures the smooth development of the first-generation special economic zones and creates the key conditions for historical miracles, which reflects the wisdom of the policymakers involved in establishing the special zones.

Consistency in thinking about the selection of space for establishing special economic zones is an important feature of the first-generation special economic zones rather than a substantive characteristic. After the chief architect of the reform and opening up, like-minded policymakers fully realized the problems and contradictions in Chinese society, and they especially clearly understood the root cause for these problems and contradictions, reforming the old system and establishing a new economic system became a strategic choice for China's development, while how to make institutional change—what path towards institutional change should be taken—was the next critical technical issue concerning reform. Calm policymakers followed Chinese culture by choosing the reform path: experiment—popularization—innovation, which was a sound path well known as "progressive reform". The first-generation special economic zones were specific strategic arrangements made on this kind of path. "Handling special cases with special methods, dealing with new matters in new ways, keeping the stance unchanged, adopting new methods" for special zones was the requirement specified by Chinese top leaders and the overall line of thought for developing special zones [1], among which "special" and "new" gave a vivid expression to institutional experimentation. Obviously, the primary task and mission for the first-generation special economic zones were institutional experiment, system and mechanism exploration rather than the development of their local areas. Shenzhen, Zhuhai, Shantou and Xiamen became four samples for such an extensive institutional experiment in China.

Another important feature of the first-generation special economic zones is "overall". This "overall"—"spatially overall" means that the establishment and development of the first-generation special economic zones served the building up of the economic system for the whole of China. In addition, their experiment was comprehensive and complicated but did not merely involve a single field. Special zones were identified by China's special zones in nature and were established by the Central Committee not by a province.[1] Apparently, being the first determines the overall nature of the first-generation special economic zones.

---

[1]Gu Mu said, "The establishment of special economic zones is a great event advocated by Comrade Deng Xiaoping, decided by the Central Committee, legalized by the Standing Committee of the National People's Congress and carried out by the State Council", see Ref. [1].

The second-generation special economic zones, represented by the Pudong New Area for development and opening-up, include the Binhai New Area of Tianjin for development and opening-up. Both areas have similar characteristics. They are significantly different from the first-generation special economic zones in the logical basis for their establishment, their basic functions and the space selection strategy.

The second-generation special zones, established in the 1990s, developed against a background that was different from that for the first-generation special zones. The biggest difference was that a consensus was reached on making a choice between the planning system and the market system and there was no dispute regarding this; more importantly, with institutional experimental exploration for more than ten years, the first-generation special zones started exporting their experience and acting as suppliers on the market system. Though the basic framework of the economic system had just developed, it was still extremely necessary for carrying out the exploration of the market system, but institutional experimentation was obviously not the primary mission for the second-generation special zones, at least not the only mission. Regional development was crucial in the functions and tasks of the second-generation special zones. The second-generation special zones were essentially designed to develop and cultivate key national strategic growth poles to produce a diffusion effect for boosting regional development so as to form new spatial developmental structures. Clearly, the establishment of national strategic growing areas was the fundamental basis for establishing the second-generation special zones. The logic for the selection of geographical locations is the same for both the Pudong New Area of Shanghai and the Binhai New Area of Tianjin. The same establishment of logic and the same basis for the selection of geographical locations enable evolution from institutional function to developmental function between the second-generation and the first-generation special economic zones.

The third-generation special economic zones, represented by Kashgar and established after 2000, include Kashgar and Zhoushan special economic zones, the early-established Wuhan, Changsha-Zhuzhou-Xiangtan pilot zones for the construction of a resource-saving and environmentally friendly society and the Chengdu-Chongqing Pilot Zone for Integrated Urban-Rural Development. Compared with the first and second-generation special economic zones, the third-generation special economic zones became diverse in the selection of their geographical locations and were no longer established on the same basis of selection. The characteristics of the geographical locations are greatly different between the westernmost Kashgar Special Zone and the eastern Zhoushan Special Zone, and among Wuhan, Chengdu-Chongqing, Changsha-Zhuzhou-Xiangtan pilot zones. Unlike the first-generation special zones, such as Shenzhen, the third-generation special zones evidently no longer aim at specific cooperation objects. All of the third-generation special economic zones were established in an issue-oriented way; for example, the Chengdu-Chongqing Pilot Zone focuses on coordinated urban-rural development; the Wuhan and the Changsha-Zhuzhou-Xiangtan pilot zones mainly involve coordinated resource and environmental development, while the Xinjiang

Kashgar Special Economic Zone centers on coordinated economic, social, cultural and political development.

The establishment and development of the third-generation special economic zones targets specific issues, while the basic task is to find solutions for specific issues such as those concerning resources and environment, rural areas, agriculture, farmers, including the overall path for addressing specific issues and regional, local solutions for specific issues.

Apparently, "well-targeted" and "specific" are the common characteristics of the third-generation special economic zones. The Kashgar Special Economic Zone is the typical example with both common characteristics. Special institutional arrangements are made to promote the economic take-off and development of Kashgar, an area with a special culture and a special geographic location, so as to boost the economic development of the whole Xinjiang area and maintain long-term peace and order.

As analyzed above, though special economic zones have existed for only 35 years in China, a developmental evolutionary process obviously marked by stages has appeared, which is a process in which the selection of spatial regions has shifted its focus from institutional experimentation to regional development to developmental issues, and the desired function has been changed from "overall" to "strategically regional" to "specifically local", with its essential connotation characterized by institutional experimentation—comprehensive practice—path exploration. China's special economic zones have dynamically evolved. Though the first-generation special economic zones, including Shenzhen and Zhuhai established 35 years ago, remain available and still exhibit the special features of the first-generation special economic zones in many fields, in other words, institutionally and in several practices, they are still designated to take up the mission of serving as the vanguard of reform, the third-generation emerging special economic zones have advanced with times to make changes not seen in their predecessors. If the dynamic evolution of the special zones is not recognized and characteristics of the times in emerging special zones are ignored, it is very likely that the strategies for developing special zones will be improper.

2 Special Economic Zones have Found Answers for Target System, Developmental Path and the Mode for Institutional Change

In the past 35 years, with institutional change experimentation as the main mission, three major issues concerning China's development were mainly stressed to push ahead with practice, make explorations and find answers in the special economic zones represented by Shenzhen.

First, explore how to establish and improve the socialist market economy target system.

The task for institutional change lies in promoting institutional evolution to achieve a new institutional balance and generate a new driving force for development between the old unequal system and the new balanced system, so as to boost social and economic development. The exchange of old and new systems in the first-generation special economic zones including Shenzhen was made possible through a series of actions, such as transfer of land based on negotiated prices, which made a breakthrough in state-owned land use and management system, the establishment of such new systems as delegation and surrender of powers, introduction of foreign capital, price reforms, the reform of the labor employment system… The reform of the economic system focused on two factors, capital and labor. Changes in the status and identity of labor in enterprise organization and the "right of freedom" brought about by these changes were the key effects of institutional reform. Merely a change in Shenzhen's land system can create miracles.

The following conclusions about the reforms in the special economic zones including Shenzhen can be drawn: first, new systems involving two factors, capital and labor, were established as substantive content from the perspective of the producer to break through the shackles imposed on capital and labor by the old system, and form specific subjects of rights including capital, land, labor and management, so as to create an incentive for factor owners, while such an incentive made it possible to change the urban economic system; second, the above reform of the system of pricing plus the establishment of a market trading system enabled the trading of factors and goods. After the institutional conditions beneficial for creating social wealth were developed, and the price reform and the trading system were put into place, the market economy could work. In my opinion, the establishment of the subject of factor property rights and a market trading system (including tangible place and intangible trading rules) constitute the basic framework for China's market economy.

Second, explore how to realize the path for mode of transformation from growth to development.

Finding new driving forces for growth to smoothly stride over "China's developmental trap" at the advent of accomplishing the mission for the growth of a labor-intensive economy is the new challenge for China. The path, built through effective practice in the special economic zones, for mode of transformation from growth to development has an important value for addressing the challenge of transformation nationwide, while such a value originates from the following connotation of transformation from economic growth to development:

1. Focus on social development. In order to encourage social development, first of all, it is necessary to provide an institutional guarantee of achieving the imbalance in social and economic development, which is an essential process of institutional change. The basic goal for China's reform, whether in rural

institutional change in the early 1980s or the subsequent reform of the urban economic system, is to create efficiency and increase the level of wealth through efficiency; therefore, such a reform is "efficiency-driven" institutional change and systems are "endogenized" in the growth process of China's economy. In the reform of special economic zones in the new period, the first priority should be given to the process of social development which is an "equity-oriented" process of institutional change, while new systems are "endogenized" in the process of social development and become an important factor in social development.

2. Focus on the quality of economic growth. Its basic point is that institutional change is made in order to alter the method for the utilization of resources, to improve the efficiency of utilization, to transform the growth mode and undertake the path towards scientific development so as to coordinate the contradictions between an increasing shortage of resources and a soaring demand.
3. Focus on coordination. Such coordination is defined at two levels: developmental coordination among regions and coordination among different fields within regions. The essential connotation of the former is that economic factors are reorganized among regions to achieve developmental integration, which refers to "spillover" development, while the latter is dominated by social, economic, cultural and environmental developmental coordination.

Third, how to transform, in institutional change, from "imported" institutional innovation based on imitation and reference to experience to self-dependent institutional innovation.

In the previous reforms, institutional change was mainly the construction of a mechanism for the operation of a market economy, which was carried out mainly by drawing upon experience from others, introducing several market means, testing and applying those market means; therefore, the key contents of institutional change were selection and introduction of a system. At the present stage, it is difficult for countries with an advanced market economy or emerging developing economies to offer available institutional choices which can meet the national conditions and the needs of institutional reform. Obviously, it is hard to finish the tasks of institutional innovation merely by means of simple learning, introduction and imitation. Institutional innovation has entered a higher level—it is more necessary to develop a set of suitable systems on the basis of existing systems, thus self-independent innovations of the systems must be emphasized. Such "self-independence" stresses "creativity". Of course, the self-independent creation of systems is by no means conducted from nothing. Reference can be made to effective international systems and mechanisms, and then systems can be reconstructed to form new systems which cater to specific needs. Inevitably, such institutional change is hard-won compared with "imported" institutional innovations.

3 The Special Economic Zones Will Still Take up Two Missions in the Future: Institutional Innovation and the First Implementation of a Developmental Path

The special economic zones underwent arduous experiments in 35 years to provide a great deal of theoretical and practical experience for national development and reform; however, subsequently, their own development was inevitably faced with two problems:

The effect of the economic growth of institutional transformation is decreasing. Like the factors which boost economic growth, such as labor and capital, systems are governed by the basic law of economics of diminishing marginal productivity. The special economic zones are the result of the institutional arrangements from a planned economic system to a new market system during China's development, and they are also the product of changing the economic system from a planned one to a market one. Initially, against the background of an extensive traditional planned system, the new market economic system can generate enough incentives for production factor owners, while these "sudden" incentives produced in a short time are in sharp contrast with the severe shortage of incentives under the planned system; as a result, the market system brings about a great contribution from marginal growth, which is commonly referred to as the institutional growth effect. However, with the gradual establishment and improvement of the market economic system in the special zones, such a "sudden" incentive effect gradually wanes and the institutional gap is also narrowed little by little, thus the attraction for investments, talents and trade declines in the process of economic growth.

Resource constraints on the special economic zones are rapidly increasing. Resources are the important factors which restrict economic development. With economic growth and an increasing population in the special zones, the scarcity of resources becomes more and more obvious, and the natural environment is also subject to increasing pressure, thus threatening the sustainable development of the economy, the population and the resources. Though scientific and technological progress can increase the rate of the utilization of the natural resources, and such factors as a gradually increasing awareness of environmental protection can enhance the population's capacity to endure, their extent is very limited. Moreover, a great number of migrant workers are flowing into the special zones, which results in lowering the overall quality of the population, as educational investments are insufficient, there is a shortage of talents, while the lack of human resources also largely affects the pace of economic build-up in the special zones and has become a bottleneck for future development. With respect to the development and the future of China's special economic zones, before the modernization of the economic system is fully finished all over China, China's special economic zones will still enjoy a sufficient basis for their existence and will still be of great practical significance; furthermore, the existence and development of China's special economic zones remains the rational path to follow towards China's modernization, and the special economic zones are heavily tasked; in order to fulfill their missions, the special economic zones need the following preconditions.

The encouragement of effective institutional innovation. Not all of the efforts towards institutional innovation can give birth to effective systems; in other words, only institutional change with a positive effect is meaningful, while institutional innovation with a zero, or even a negative, effect is ineffective change; such a reform wastes social resources and makes the society sustain reform costs. It is not easy to initiate ineffective institutional reform under a mechanism of induced change since institutional changes are based on social needs and are well-targeted, while it is easy to incur ineffective reform in a government-led compulsory mechanism of institutional evolution due to political achievements or to a lack of knowledge and information available to the executors of the reforms. If an emphasis is placed on merely the act of "change" rather than the effect of "change", this will certainly substantially reduce the effect of institutional reform.

The provision of adequate reform incentives. After a contract system with remuneration linked to output was implemented, the growth of land output highly incentivized the farmers stricken by widespread poverty, which was the cause for rapidly popularizing rural economic reform and bearing fruit. Afterwards, the state-owned reform of the economy, characterized by delegation and surrender of powers, made operators and employees share reform interests, thus delivering considerable incentives for urban residents with low wages. Meanwhile, the introduction of foreign capital and the development of the private economy greatly increased the average profit of capital owners; consequentially, innumerable villagers migrated from rural areas to cities in order to share city civilization and obtain more-than-expected labor returns, thus the incentives from reform were sufficient. Today's reforms in the special economic zones require institutional reform interests and interest sharing mechanism greatly different from that in previous reforms. With respect to institutional innovations that promote social development and institutional designs that transform the economic growth mode, boost the coordination of social, economic and environmental development, narrow the social developmental gap, etc., their change process is of a public welfare nature. The process of institutional innovation is also fraught with risks. The reform process involves adjustment of the existing interest pattern, giving rise to high reform costs. When governments are the subjects of reform, local governments are system creators and executors for the creation of specific institutional contents within the framework of the reform developed by the Central Government; subject to the above reform interests and costs, as system innovators, local governments are vulnerable to insufficient incentives for reform acts. Therefore, continuous institutional practice and practice regarding the path in the special zones requires the Central Government to grant local governments with the right to innovate systems, and an evaluation mechanism for the effect of the reform, a mechanism for the removal of reform risks, a performance reward and a compensation mechanism for effective reform, etc., should be developed to incentivize local officials to carry out reforms. A continuous incentive mechanism is the prerequisite for pushing ahead with reforms according to the plan.

It is more important to explore repeatable institutional contents. In the Binhai New Area of Tianjin and the Pudong New Area of Shanghai, reforms were concretized into urban developmental strategies and measures long ago, such as reforms in financial enterprises, financial business, the financial market and financial deregulation, the investment system, the administrative management system, etc. in the Binhai New Area of Tianjin; reform priorities including the transformation of the economic operational mode and the corresponding concrete actions in the Pudong New Area, e.g. the establishment of the "National Pilot Intellectual Property Park", taking the lead in developing pledge business of intellectual property rights, the establishment of the tribunal of conciliation and arbitration for intellectual property disputes, etc. With regard to the motive force for development, the special economic zones have transformed their motive force from policy innovations to institutional innovations.

All of the special economic zones, including today's free trade zones, have been seeking to fulfill the historical mission of proving experience and of becoming models for national reform and development; thus their primary task involves general systems, mechanisms and developmental methods that are of a higher level, are more universal or adoptable and are based on their own development. Only in this way can the reform, first implementation and experimentation in the special economic zones be more valuable for national development.

The unique basic feature of the special economic zones is their advantage over the hinterland in carrying out a market economic system during development. The existence of special economic zones is based on the institutional difference between China's traditional economic system and the market economic system and on the full recognition of the efficiency of wealth creation of the market economic system. The basic framework for China's market economy was basically established nationwide over the past 35 years. However, China's market economic system is still underdeveloped, thus the task for the special economic zones as "institutional experimental sites" has not yet been accomplished. For the future of China's special economic zones, before the complete modernization of China's economic system is fully finished, the special economic zones will still have a sufficient basis for their existence and will still be of great practical significance, and the existence and development of China's special economic zones will still be the rational path to undertake in order to achieve the modernization of China. There is still a long way to go for the future development of China's special economic zones amid new issues concerning national development.

References

1. Shi Chunmiao: A Record of Actions for Seeking a Delegation of Powers from the Central Government to the Shenzhen Special Economic Zone at the Early Stage of Reform and Opening-up, *HongGuangJiao*, 2010(9).

The Course, Achievements and Inspirations of the Reform and Opening-Up of the Shenzhen Special Economic Zone

Zhong Jian

Abstract The history of the Shenzhen Special Economic Zone epitomizes the full story of China's reform and opening up. The Shenzhen Special Economic Zone is the important product of China's reform and opening up and also the important achievement made in China's reform and opening up. Carefully summing up the practice and experience of Shenzhen's reform and opening up is of great historical and practical significance.

Keywords Shenzhen special economic zone · Reform and opening-up · Experience · Inspirations

Remarkable achievements have been made in various aspects in Shenzhen, and rare miracles have been created in the world's history of industrialization, urbanization and modernization since 1980 when the special economic zones were officially established. Shenzhen is one of the special economic zones established in the earliest period in China and also the best, most influential special zone. The material wealth and the spiritual wealth created in Shenzhen, and even Shenzhen's contributions to the whole country, are tremendous and amazing, thus Shenzhen deserves to be written about elaborately. Undoubtedly, carefully reviewing and summarizing the history and experience of the Shenzhen Special Economic Zone in the reform and opening up is of great realistic and historical significance.

Zhong Jian (1965–) Professor, Doctoral Supervisor, College of Economics, Shenzhen University, mainly engaged in research on China's and foreign special economic zones.

Z. Jian (✉)
College of Economics, Shenzhen University, Shenzhen 518060, China

Y. Yuan (ed.), *Studies on China's Special Economic Zones*, Research Series on the Chinese Dream and China's Development Path,
DOI 10.1007/978-981-10-3704-7_3

1 Historical Review of the Course of the Reform and Opening-Up in Shenzhen

The Shenzhen Special Economic Zone was established and developed as the first implementation zone and experimental zone for reform and opening up against the general historical background of carrying out the reform and opening up policy and hastening the modernization of China. In fact, the developmental history of the Shenzhen Special Economic Zone covers the whole process of reform and opening up.

(I) The stage of establishment, laying of the foundation, local reform and opening up (1978–1985)

The Third Plenary Session of the 11th Central Committee of the Communist Party of China held, in December, 1978, a session of great historical significance, which heralded in a new period in the history of reform and opening up. As a matter of fact, the Baoan Area, adjacent to Hong Kong and from which many people fled to Hong Kong, became one of the top concerns of the Central Government and Guangdong Province in 1977 and 1978. Deng Xiaoping inspected Guangdong Province in November, 1977. When leaders of the Party Committee of Guangdong Province reported that the problem that farmers in some border areas were fleeing to Hong Kong was quite impressive, Deng Xiaoping said that the problems that were being faced were relatively concentrated and clear-cut, that a report should be delivered to the Central Government, the problems should be analyzed and specified into those which should be solved by Guangdong Province, by other provinces and by the Central Government, respectively; in my opinion, the central problem was a policy problem. In April, 1978, the Central Government sent an economic and trade delegation to Hong Kong and Macau for an on-the-spot survey; afterwards, the delegation submitted "A Survey Report on Hong Kong and Macau's Economy", and suggested that Baoan County and Zhuhai County, adjacent to Hong Kong and Macau respectively, should be designated as export bases and should be gradually built into outward-looking production bases, processing bases at a high level and tourism areas for attracting tourists from Hong Kong and Macau. In February, 1979, the State Council approved and forwarded the "Report on the Foreign Trade Base and Municipal Construction Plan for Baoan County and Zhuhai County" as prepared by Guangdong Province, and required Shenzhen and Zhuhai to be built into export-oriented commodity bases towards Hong Kong and Macau, tourism areas for attracting tourists from Hong Kong and Macau and new border cities, all to be done within 3–5 years. In April, 1979, the Central Government convened a working meeting and officially vowed to establish pilot export-oriented special zones and take special policies and flexible measures for Guangdong Province and Fujian Province. In July, 1979, the Central Government approved and forwarded two reports of Guangdong Province and Fujian Province on foreign economic activities and flexible measures, and decided to establish pilot special zones in Shenzhen, Zhuhai, Shantou and Xiamen. In May, 1980, the Central Government approved and forwarded the Meeting Minutes of Guangdong Province and Fujian Province, and instructed Guangdong Province to first concentrate various forces on building the Shenzhen Special Zone, and adopted the suggestion of Guangdong Province that the "Special Export Zone" should be renamed the "Special Economic Zone". In August, 1980, the Regulations of Guangdong Province on Special Economic Zones were passed in the 15th Session of the Standing Committee of the National People's Congress, which marked the official establishment of special economic zones, including Shenzhen.

Construction was started on the Shenzhen Special Economic Zone the earliest among four special economic zones. First, in Shenzhen, the Shekou Industrial Zone was built in 1979, and large-scale infrastructure construction began in 1980 when Luohu and Shangbu urban areas were developed, and ports including Shekou, Chiwan, Dongjiaotou, Mawan, etc. were built. A number of industrial zones were developed and built. Massive foreign capital and advanced technologies were introduced. Industrial construction commenced. The construction of eight large cultural facilities including Shenzhen University (1983) and libraries began. The cultural undertaking was launched and on its way. The overall plan for urban construction, economic and social development was developed. The administrative system of the special zone was gradually improved. Relevant supporting laws and regulations were made. Second, with the capital construction management system and a reform of the pricing system as the breakthrough, market-oriented reforms were first initiated nationwide in the wage system (1979), the capital construction system (1980), the labor employment system (1980), the pricing system (1982), the enterprise system (1983), the labor insurance system (1983), the cadre and personnel system (1982) and government agencies (1981), etc. Third, the Shekou Industrial Zone (1979) was founded; Shatoujiao (1983) was opened as the window for the opening up; ports including Wenjindu (1978), Shekou Port (1981), Meisha (1984), Shatoujiao (1984), Chiwan (1984) and Daya Bay (1985) were successively opened. The financial industry was deregulated to introduce a number of overseas banks. Fourth, such philosophies as "Time is Money, Efficiency is Life" (1983) were put forward, and "Shenzhen Speed" at which it took only three days to build three storeys (1984) was achieved, which drove, stimulated and boosted reform, the opening up and modernization nationwide. The reforms in this period were mainly characterized by carrying out local reforms, making single breakthroughs, promoting reforms by the opening up. These reforms broke the fetters of the original planned economic system, removed certain obstacles for reform, opening up, the construction and development of special zones, and produced a demonstration effect on reforms of the urban economic system nationwide. Of course, there were also severe tests from smuggling incidents in the first half of 1982 and a historic event that Deng Xiaoping inspected Shenzhen Special Economic Zone in 1984. Deng Xiaoping pointed out that the special economic zones served as the windows for technologies, management, knowledge and opening up. He stated that the development and practice of Shenzhen proved that our policy for establishing special economic zones was correct. He also said that one guiding thought for our establishing special economic zones and implementing the opening-up policy should be clear-cut: we should open up rather than close off.

(II) The stage of the development of economic transformation, all-round reform and opening up (1986–1992)

As from the end of 1984, the whole of China witnessed a new round of macroeconomic fluctuation, leading to the release of comprehensive tightening policies. The Shenzhen Special Economic Zone faced a tightening monetary policy, economic difficulties resulting from cutting down on capital construction and the debate on whether the developmental direction for the special zone was correct. From the end of 1985 to the beginning of 1986, the State Council convened a working meeting on the special zones in Shenzhen, and required the Shenzhen Special Economic Zone to shift its work priorities from previous extensive construction and laying of the foundation to an emphasis on production, an increase of level and the pursuit of benefits, a focus on industry, integration of industry, trade and technology, comprehensive development, a striving to develop a knowledge-intensive, technology-intensive, industry-focused outward-looking special economic zone. As from 1986, the Shenzhen Special Economic Zone entered a new stage at which an outward-looking economy was developed outside the planned economic system and a market-oriented economic reform was carried out in an all-round way.

First, with respect to the opening up, (1) foreign capital and technologies were utilized to build Chiwan Port, Shekou Port, Dongjiaotou Wharf, Shekou Oil Depot, local telephone works, Shajiao B Power Plant, Overseas Chinese Town (1986), Daya Bay Nuclear Power (1987) and the Guangzhou-Shenzhen Expressway (1987) and other infrastructures; (2) investment promotion was intensified, overseas capital and technologies were used to vigorously develop "the three-processing and one compensation"[1] enterprises and "three kinds of foreign-related enterprises"[2]; (3) trans-regional, cross-industry, multi-tier, multi-mode horizontal integration with the hinterland was actively conducted, and a large number of inland associated enterprises were built to cover the shortage of capital, technologies and talents, becoming one of the important forces for Shenzhen's economic development; (4) cooperation with the Chinese Academy of Sciences was carried out to set up a

[1]"The three-processing and one compensation" means the processing of materials supplied by foreign clients, processing according to buyer's samples, the assembling of parts supplied by foreign clients and compensation trade—an enterprise trade mode tentatively created on the Chinese Mainland at the beginning of the reform and opening up.

[2]Chinese-foreign joint ventures, Chinese-foreign cooperative enterprises and wholly foreign-owned enterprises established within China are called "three kinds of foreign-related enterprises".

science and technology industrial park (1985), starting the development of high and new technology industries; (5) two bonded industrial zones including Shatoujiao (1987) and Futian (1991) were created to promote the development of an outward-looking economy; (6) a number of backbone foreign trade enterprises were established to actively develop entrepot trade and ocean trade; (7) Mawan Wharf (1990), Huanggang Port (1991), Yantian Port (1992) and Shenzhen Airport (1991) were opened. This series of opening-up measures were taken to rapidly form an outward-looking economy which was dominated by industry and combined industry with trade. In 1987, Shenzhen's export trade was larger than its import trade, reversing its trade deficit. In 1988, Shenzhen ranked No. 2 among large and medium-sized cities nationwide in terms of total exports. Shenzhen topped the list of large and medium-sized cities nationwide in the total volume of import and export trade as from 1992. In 1987, Deng Xiaoping said that recently Shenzhen's products at a relatively technological level were able to enter the international market; the success of the opening-up policy lay in this, this was the real success.

Second, reform of the market-oriented economic system was promoted across the board. In order to quicken the development of the special zone and the introduction of foreign capital, the Shenzhen Municipal Party Committee vowed to shift local reforms of the special zone to a comprehensive reform, switch from single reforms to a systematic reform, and from preliminary reforms to in-depth reforms so as to gradually develop in a supporting, comprehensive, all-round direction. Major reform measures: (1) the first action was taken to launch a reform of the joint-stock system of state-owned enterprises (1986), to innovate the state-owned asset management system (1987), to put into practice the enterprise contracting system, the stockholding system, the transfer of property rights and bankruptcy, etc. (2) the financial system was reformed to build a multi-tier, outward-looking financial market, including the introduction of foreign banks (1982), the establishment of regional joint-stock banks including China Merchants Bank (1987) and Shenzhen Development Bank (1987); the first foreign exchange swap center was established in China (1988); the non-ferrous metals futures market was established (1991); shares were issued to the public (1987); the securities exchange was established (1990); (3) a breakthrough was made in the traditional management system for state-owned land, with public land auctions carried out for the first time (1987); (4) the housing system was reformed (the commodity house, the scanty profit house, the welfare-oriented house systems were carried out) to gradually commercialize houses (1988); (5) institutions were adjusted and a pilot reform of the civil servant system was conducted (1988); (6) the reform of the labor and wage system was intensified, the labor contract system was adopted and the social security system was established (1986). The main characteristics of this stage were supporting reforms and comprehensive promotion. With these reforms, the framework of the old system was basically broken up, and the economic system and operating mechanism dominated by market regulation and supplemented by planned regulation preliminarily took shape. In 1988, the State Council gave its approval for Shenzhen to be specifically designated in the state plan, and gave provincial-level economic management authority to Shenzhen. In 1992, the Standing Committee of the National People's Congress delegated the Shenzhen Municipal People's Congress and its Standing Committee and the Municipal Government the power to make local laws and regulations.

In this period, Shenzhen's economy took off, industrialization accelerated, urban construction advanced rapidly, and the GDP grew by an annual 30% on average and hit 5 billion yuan, 10 billion yuan in 1987 and 1989 respectively, while the roles of the "four windows" became further evident. In the spring of 1992, Deng Xiaoping confirmed the tremendous achievements in reform, the opening up and the construction of the special economic zones, and stated that the achievements in the construction of Shenzhen had given these people a definite answer: Special economic zones were socialist, not capitalist. Meanwhile, great events such as the "Shekou Brainstorm" in 1988 and the "Stock Incident" in 1992 occurred.

(III) The stage of increasing its advantages and of creating new ones, achieving a great leap forward in development (1993–2002)

Marked by Deng Xiaoping's South Talks[3] and the 14th National Congress of the Communist Party of China, the development of the Shenzhen Special Economic Zone entered a new period during which the focal point was shifted from preferential policies given to the special economic zones by the Central Government in the past to quality improvement, the increase in and creation of new advantages. The 2nd Shenzhen Municipal Congress of the Communist Party of China confirmed efforts to make strategic adjustments and achieve three fundamental transformations: first, transform from the traditional planned economic system to the socialist market economy system; second, transform from the extensive economic growth mode to the intensive economic growth mode; third, transform the focal point from special policies to quality improvement, the increase in and creation of new advantages in order to develop the special zones. In 2000, the 3rd Shenzhen Municipal Congress of the Communist Party of China specified the goal for increasing and creating new advantages, scaling new heights to first basically achieve modernization by fostering more new advantages in institutional innovations, expansion of the opening-up, industrial upgrading, urban functions, law-based city governance so as to build Shenzhen into a model socialist city with Chinese characteristics.

In institutional reform, Shenzhen specified the goal for being the first area in the nation to establish a socialist market economy system. In order to reach such a goal, continued bold experimentations were made in developing a modern enterprise system, improving the market system, transforming governmental functions, perfecting the social security system and building a law and regulation system adapted to a market economy, so as to preliminarily form the basic framework for a socialist

[3]From January 18 to February 21, 1992, Deng Xiaoping inspected Wuchang, Shenzhen, Zhuhai and Shanghai, etc. and delivered a series of important speeches, called Deng Xiaoping's South Talks.

market economy system. First, the reform of state-owned enterprises was intensified and a modern enterprise system was established (1994); second, the reform of the state-owned asset management system was intensified and a three-level state-owned asset supervision and operation mechanism was developed (1992); third, the ownership structure was improved and the development of a private economy was promoted (2003); fourth, commercial and trade reform was intensified, and innovations were made in the financial business and system, and a foreign exchange broking center was established (1994), a property rights exchange market was built (1993), a technology market was developed (1993), a venture capital investment market was cultivated (2002), the labor market was improved and a modern market system was continuously enhanced; fifth, the transformation of government functions was intensified (items subject to examination and approval were reduced or cancelled, 1998), a reform of the fiscal system was promoted (1996), the reform of the governmental procurement system was carried forward (1998), the reform of the investment and financing system was quickened (2001), the building of a credit system was strengthened (2002), a macro-control system was continuously improved; sixth, the reform of the distribution system was widened and an annual salary system for enterprise operators was applied (1997), the distribution system combining work-based distribution with distribution based on production factors was adopted (2002); seventh, the comprehensive reform of the social insurance system was launched, medical insurance, endowment insurance and housing accumulation fund systems were carried out (1992), a work-related injury insurance system was adopted (1993), and a pilot medical reform combining social pooling with individual accounts was initiated (1995). Eighth, law-based city governance was carried out in an all-round way, and reform of the administrative system was promoted, including the intensification of organizational reform and the implementation of nine legalizations (2001); the reform of civil servant management system was promoted and national public servant system was comprehensively implemented (1993); ninth, grass-roots democratic construction was boosted (1993), the judicial system was reformed (2001) and the system for fighting corruption, keeping government clean and preventing corruption was built, etc. In July, 1992, the Standing Committee of the National People's Congress made a decision about delegating the powers to make laws and regulations to the Shenzhen Municipal People's Congress and its Standing Committee and the Shenzhen Municipal People's Government.

Actions were taken to further increase the level of the opening up and become compatible with internationally accepted practices. First, attention was paid to the quality of the introduced foreign capital and the technical content of products; priority was given to introducing high-tech and knowledge-intensive enterprises. Hong Kong Hutchison Whampoa was introduced to build the Yantian Port (1993); the Yantian Port was opened (1992); Shenzhen Airport's port was opened (1993); foreign capital and technologies were utilized to build the Daya Bay Nuclear Power Plant (1994). Second, the foreign investment service center (1995) and the foreign investor complaints center (2001) were established; Shenzhen became the first to give a national treatment to foreign investors and foreigners (1996); services for foreign investors were improved and the level of the utilization of foreign capital was continuously increased. Third, the reform of the port system was intensified. International practices were followed in order to push ahead with major reforms of the port system and further simplify examination and inspection procedures (1992); a unified customs declaration was created and one-stop services were provided at Wenjindu Port, Huanggang Port and Shatoujiao Port (1994); pilot 24-h-customs clearance was carried out and a centralized application for inspection was put into practice at Huanggang Port (1994); foreigners who toured Hong Kong and then came to Shenzhen enjoyed 72 h visa-free treatment (1994); examination and inspection methods were reformed at ports and the procedure for declaration, examination and inspection at access roads for vehicles was canceled (1995). Fourth, foreign trade was further expanded by implementing the Going Global policy and developing an international market, increasing the quality and level of foreign trade and boosting the sustained growth of foreign trade. Fifth, Shenzhen-Hong Kong investment and trade cooperation was actively promoted (at the end of 2002, cumulative actually-utilized Hong Kong capital amounted to 18,884 million USD, there were 9244 Hong Kong-funded enterprises, exports to Hong Kong reached 20,008 million USD); there was infrastructure and port cooperation (expansion of Yantian Port, treatment and improvement of Shenzhen River), cooperation regarding the financial service industry (the Shenzhen Expressway was listed in Hong Kong in 1997, two-way settlement business involving the Hong Kong dollar cheque was launched in 2002, real-time foreign currency payment was made) and cooperation concerning tourism (144 h facilitation measures were implemented in 2001), etc.

During this period, Shenzhen witnessed a great leap forward in the development of the economy, and suddenly a vigorous development of the high and new technology industry, the modern logistics industry and the modern financial industry which became three pillar industries; moreover, there was continuous improvement of urban functions, and all-round progress was made in various undertakings in the society, as well as a substantial improvement in people's lives. The annual economic growth rate remained about 20% on average, and Shenzhen's total output value hit 100 billion yuan (1994), 200 billion yuan (1998), 300 billion yuan (2002); the cumulative amount that was turned over to the central finances was 366.3 billion yuan, and Shenzhen was in the front rank of large and medium-sized cities nationwide in terms of comprehensive economic strength. Meanwhile, the Qingshuihe Explosion occurred in 1993, and the prospects for the special zone were widely debated in 1995.

(IV) The stage of the intensification of reforms and the opening up, all-round development (2003–Now)

As the new century arrived, Shenzhen saw great changes in the development situation and environment, and faced a grim reality that land, energy resources, population and the ecological environment had become unsustainable and social contradictions were acute. In 2003, Hu Jintao inspected Shenzhen and required

Shenzhen to accelerate its development, to develop first, to develop in a coordinated way, and to continue to advance at the forefront of the country. In 2003, the Shenzhen Municipal Party Committee put forward the strategic goal of building an internationalized city. In 2005, the Shenzhen Municipal Party Committee set forth the goal for building a "harmonious Shenzhen", an "efficiency-focused Shenzhen", comprehensively develop an outlook on scientific development, with new achievements made in reforms, the opening up, as well as in economic and social development. Shenzhen successively implemented the strategy for building a culturally advanced city and a self-dependent strategy of innovation.

In parallel with the intensification of reforms in the economic and administrative system, Shenzhen also advanced in the institutional reforms in social and cultural fields. First, reform of the state-owned enterprises was continuously intensified by transferring part of the shares of municipal state-owned enterprises, including the energy, water, gas and bus groups, as well as food corporations, preliminarily diversifying the property rights of state-owned enterprises (2003); the State-owned Assets Supervision and Administration Commission was established to comprehensively perform the duties of supervising personnel, matters and assets (2004), and the state-owned asset supervision system was improved; the reform of the labor, personnel and distribution systems of enterprises was intensified (2006), and measures were adopted to put the enterprise operation mechanism fully in line with the market. Second, the recycling economy was promoted in an all-round way, as well as the construction of a resource saving and environmentally friendly society (2006). Third, the reform of administrative system was intensified and the Industrial Association Service Agency (2004), the Reform Office (2005), the Municipal Government Service Hall (2004) were established, and e-government affairs were launched; moreover, the examination and approval system for major investment projects was reformed (2006), and the construction of a modern service-oriented government was accelerated. Fourth, urbanization was quickened to turn Shenzhen into the first city in China without a rural administration organizational system (2004). Fifth, the reform of the cultural system was intensified by reorganizing the newspaper, broadcasting and TV and distribution groups, and by holding the Cultural Industry Fair, thus speeding up the development of the cultural industry (2004). Sixth, the reform of public institutions was boosted, and the employee system was put into practice (2005). Seventh, the reform of the scientific and technological management system was promoted, and a national innovation-oriented city was built. Eighth, the reforms of the social management system (2004) and the social security system were intensified, the People's Net Welfare Index System was introduced (2006), and the public service system was continuously improved, and efforts were intensified towards improving people's well-being.

With regard to the reform and opening up, first, supporting industrial advantages and an excellent logistics environment were utilized to attract more world-famous corporations, large projects, core manufacturing segments, research and development centers, regional headquarters and purchasing centers of multinational corporations to Shenzhen, and the headquarters economy was vigorously developed. Second, high-end projects of the new high-tech industrial chain was introduced, and investment promotion in automobiles and parts, fine chemical and equipment manufacturing fields was intensified: also, the reform and opening up in commercial, financial, logistics, telecommunications and professional service fields were steadily promoted. Third, the strategy for diversifying export markets and vitalizing trade by science and technology was implemented, and more efforts were made to develop emerging markets including Russia, the Middle East, South America and Africa while expanding those of the USA, the EU and Japan. Enterprises were actively encouraged to go global, and an overseas marketing network was established to carry out overseas processing trade, project contracting, and to forge strategic alliances with foreign multinational corporations, as well as to press ahead with the international operation of enterprises and cultivate local multinational corporations. Fourth, the Shenzhen-Hong Kong cooperation was continued at a higher level, and the Shenzhen-Hong Kong "1 + 8" cooperation agreement (2004), the "Shenzhen-Hong Kong Innovation Circles" cooperation agreement (2007) and the Shenzhen-Hong Kong "1 + 6" cooperation agreement (2007) were signed; moreover, Shenzhen Bay and Futian Port were opened (2007), the construction of cross-border large infrastructure was quickened, and cooperation and communication was conducted in port customs clearance, in the new and hi-tech industry, the financial industry, the modern service industry and tourism, airports, education, science and technology, etc. Regional cooperation with the Pearl River Delta and Pan-Pearl-River Delta Region was actively pursued; CEPA and the "9 + 2" cooperation framework were implemented at a higher speed so as to maximize the hinterland and space for Shenzhen's development.

2 Historic Achievements in Shenzhen in 28 Years of Practice

(I) The Astonishing "Shenzhen Speed" for economic development has been created

With construction and development for 28 years, Shenzhen has developed from a backward border town in the past to a flourishing modern city, where its economic strength was among the top of large and medium-sized cities nationwide and a rare industrialization, urbanization and modernization speed was created. Its GDP rose from 196 million yuan to 676,541 million yuan during the period 1979–2007, it ranked No.4 among large and medium-sized cities nationwide, an annual increase of 31.20%; per-capita GDP soared from 606 yuan to 79,221 yuan (10,628 USD), ranking No. 1, an annual increase of 17.64%. Total fixed asset investments skyrocketed from 59 million yuan to 134.5 billion yuan, an annual increase of 29.40%. The total volume of import and export trade increased from 17 million USD to 287,533 million USD, ranking No. 1, an annual increase of 38.34%. Total exports grew from 9 million USD to 168,493 million USD, ranking No. 1 for 15 consecutive years, an annual increase of 38.81%. Fiscal revenue within the local budget soared from 17 million yuan to 65,806 million yuan, ranking No. 3, an annual increase of 31.70%. The amount turned over to the central finance was 211.2 billion yuan in 2007.

(II) Remarkable progress has been made in industrial transformation and upgrading

Shenzhen has been transformed from a city dominated by trade, real estate, "the three-processing and one compensation" to a city with the highest output value of new high-tech products and the largest export volume in China during the period 1980–2007. The structure of the primary, secondary and tertiary industries developed from 28.9: 26.0: 45.1 to 0.1: 50.9: 49.0; industrial ecology and economic structure changed profoundly. The high and new technology industry rapidly rose, with the product output value from the high and new technology industry reaching 759.88 billion yuan in 2007, accounting for 56.89% of the total above-scale industrial output value in the whole city, in which the products based on proprietary intellectual property rights made up more than 58%. The modern service industry dominated by logistics, information, finance and culture was booming. The added value from the financial industry hit 75 billion yuan in 2007, accounting for 11.6% of the GDP. The added value realized in the logistics industry stood at 65,422 million yuan, accounting for 9.67% of the GDP. The cultural industry rapidly developed. A number of backbone cultural sectors including the press and publications, advertising, cultural product manufacturing, cultural entertainment, sports, cultural tourism, radio, film and television took shape, among which printing, media and cultural tourism took the leading positions nationwide; the added value from the cultural industry accounted for 6.7% of the GDP. In coordination with four pillar industries, highly influential industrial fairs, including the China Hi-tech Fair, the Financial Expo, the Logistics Fair and the Cultural Industry Fair, were held.

(III) It has become second to none in China in the outward-looking degree of its economy

The quality and level of opening up in the Shenzhen Special Economic Zone were on the rise. In 2007, the total volume of import and export trade was 287,533 million USD, among which total exports stood at 168,493 million USD, accounting for 13.83 and 45.63% of the total national exports and total exports from Guangdong Province respectively, making it No. 1 among large and medium-sized cities nationwide for 15 consecutive years. Foreign investors from more than 90 countries and territories invested in Shenzhen; there were 36,984 foreign direct investment projects. A total of 148 global top 500 companies established a commercial presence in Shenzhen. Cumulative contractual foreign capital and cumulative actually-utilized foreign capital reached 63,138 million USD and 37,431 million USD, respectively. A total of 8,313,000 person-time overnight overseas tourists were received. Foreign exchange earnings from international tourists stood at 2623 million USD. Shenzhen's enterprises actively participated in the global economy. As of the end of 2006, 367 overseas enterprises and organizations were established, and cumulative investments were nearly 1.5 billion USD, covering more than 80 countries and territories. In 2007, new contracts concerning contracted projects in foreign countries and labor service cooperation amounted to 2985 million USD. Meanwhile, regional economic cooperation with Hong Kong, the Pearl River Delta, inland provinces and municipalities was increasingly intensified so as to boost regional resource integration, advantage complementation and common development.

(IV) The capability for independent innovation has been increasingly enhanced

The output value of new high-tech products has increased by 46.5% on average and the number of patent applications has rapidly risen by more than 30% since 1992. The proportion of the output value from new high-tech products based on proprietary intellectual property rights has exceeded 58%. Huawei and ZTE have grown into leading self-dependent innovation enterprises with transnational operations, while small and medium-sized innovative companies, including Tencent, Netac, Mindray, etc., have become the leading enterprises in relevant fields. There are more than 0.8 million professional and technical talents, more than 700 research and development institutions, including nearly 70 foreign-funded research and development centers. More than 90% of the research and development institutions are established in enterprises. More than 90% of the research and development funds come from enterprises. More than 90% of the research and development personnel are concentrated in enterprises. More than 90% of service invention patents originate in enterprises, thus enterprises have really become the main body of self-dependent innovation. In 2007, the number of patent applications in Shenzhen reached 35,808, which ranked No. 2 among large and medium-sized cities nationwide, among which there were 19,198 invention patent applications, accounting for 53.6% of the total patent applications in Shenzhen, which ranked No.1 among large and medium-sized cities nationwide, making up 71.9% of the total number of patent applications in Guangdong Province. Foreign patent applications dramatically increased, and there were 2480 PCT international patent applications, which accounted for 45.9% of the total national number, and ranked No. 1 nationwide for four consecutive years. Currently, there are 76 Chinese famous brands which rank No. 1 nationwide, and 3 Chinese world famous brands which account for 30% of the total national number, ranking No. 1 nationwide. A relatively complete regional innovation system, which is market-oriented, aims at industrialization, is dominated by enterprises and enables the close integration of the government, industry, universities, research institutions, capital and intermediaries, has taken shape in Shenzhen.

(V) Outstanding achievements have been made in urban construction modernization

Modernization and internationalization have been adopted as a standard; the urban infrastructure system and the comprehensive transport system have been increasingly improved. The level of urban management has continually increased. Its function as a regional central economic city has been greatly enhanced, and it has become a modern, international livable metropolis with complete functions and a beautiful environment. At present, Shenzhen is the only city with sea, land and air ports in China. Shenzhen boasts a modern three-dimensional transportation network. Its international airport offers 18 international flight routes and 90 domestic flight routes, and it has become the fourth largest airport in China, with a passenger throughput of 18.36 million person-times. Currently, there are 152 port berths in Shenzhen, including 61 berths above 10,000 t. Port container throughput is 18.47 million TEUs and ranks No.4 in the world. Luohu Port, Huanggang Port and Yantian Port are the largest land passenger transport port, the largest land freight transport port and the largest container seaport in China, respectively. The post and telecommunication industry has rapidly developed. In Shenzhen, there are 5,077,900 land-line telephone subscribers and 14.94 million mobile telephone subscribers; each 100 people own 221 telephones (including mobile telephones) on average. The built-up area covers an area of 719 km^2. The green coverage ratio in built-up area reaches 45.0%. The treatment rate of domestic sewage is 65.2%. The rate of water, reaching the standard, from reservoirs as main sources of drinking water, hits 98.11%. The rate of popularization of tap water reaches 99.9%. The rate of comprehensive utilization of industrial solid wastes is 81.76%. Shenzhen was awarded the title of "Model City for Environmental Protection" by the State in 1997. Shenzhen was granted the title of international "Garden City" in 2000. It was given the China Habitat Environment Prize in 2001. It was listed among the first batch of "National Civilized Cities" in 2005. It has also been awarded many honors including the "National Garden City", the "UN Habitat Scroll of Honor Award", the "Sir Leslie Patrick Abercrombie Honorary Award", etc.

(VI) The people's living standard has been substantially improved

With rapid economic development, the citizens' level of income and quality of life have been elevated in an all-round way, and the consumption structure and living environment have been improved day by day, resulting in a leap from adequate food and clothing to affluence. At the end of 2007, the permanent population was 8,615,500, among which the population with registered permanent residence was 2,123,800. Urban per capita disposable income reached 24,870.21 yuan. Per capita consumption expenditure of its residents was 18,752.87 yuan. The urban Engel coefficient was 32.5%. Year-end per capita housing building area of residents was 24.47 m^2. A multi-tier social security system took shape in the whole city, with an increasing coverage and a gradually enhanced guarantee capability. At the year-end, 4,939,700 people, 1,796,200 people and 2,805,500 people were covered by basic endowment insurance, unemployment insurance and basic medical insurance, respectively. Various undertakings, including education, health and culture, flourished. New progress was made in spiritual civilization and political civilization.

3 Inspirations from the Successes in Shenzhen Special Economic Zone

The successes in the Shenzhen Special Economic Zone represent a miracle not only in the developmental history of the world's special economic zones but also in the history of the development of the world's cities. The practice and achievements in the Shenzhen Special Economic Zone go beyond the practice and experience in special economic zones in foreign countries, and its significance is not confined within the limits of the special zone itself. It has Chinese characteristics and the significance of innovation for the world. Shenzhen has accumulated valuable experience for a drive towards national reform, opening-up and modernization. Shenzhen has also made important contributions to the exploration of the socialist road with Chinese characteristics. First, it has served as the "experimental field" in institutional reform. Second, it has played an important role as a "window" in the opening up. Third, it has acted as a "demonstration zone" in construction modernization. Fourth, it has played an important role in promoting the smooth return of Hong Kong and Macau to the motherland, and maintaining their prosperity and stability. The successful practice in the Shenzhen Special Economic Zone at least offers the following beneficial inspirations for us.

(I) Emancipating the mind is the important magic weapon for developing socialism with Chinese characteristics

Comrade Deng Xiaoping stated that once the target was clear, we should make bold attempts and breakthroughs, the important experience from Shenzhen lay in being courageous to break through. This explained the secret of the successes in the Shenzhen Special Economic Zone and a profound principle. First, we should emancipate our mind; second, we should be bold in practice. This is also the fundamental point of the successful experience in the practical construction of the Shenzhen Special Economic Zone. Each major step for Shenzhen's reform, opening up and construction modernization is nothing but the result of emancipating the mind and taking bold actions to make breakthroughs. Emancipating the mind, making brave attempts and breakthroughs in Shenzhen brought about a new path and a new pattern for development, thus Shenzhen became a banner for national the reform and opening up. The practice in the Shenzhen Special Economic Zone can provide the following inspirations: first, we should be bolder and dare to experiment in reform and opening up. Reform is the second revolution at an unprecedented degree. Opening-up means risks. This requires the courage and boldness to be the first to make attempts. We should never fear in face of any risk and should not be bewildered by any interference. Second, emancipating the mind is the key to utilizing policies well and in a sufficient, flexible way. In the reform and opening up, we should boldly make breakthroughs and modify inappropriate laws, regulations and policies, and we should carry out the feasible reform and opening-up measures in a bolder, more resolute and creative way. Third, emphasis should be placed on practice in reform and opening up. The achievements in the Shenzhen Special

Economic Zone were made through concrete actions rather than debate. Fourth, we should allow experiments and errors. Pushing ahead with reform and opening up, building special zones is experimental and aims at exploring the socialist road with Chinese characteristics.

(II) Reform and opening up is the only road to emancipate and develop productive social forces

The fundamental cause for making great changes in Shenzhen's economy and society lies in the reform and opening up. The Shenzhen Special Economic Zone could not have come into being and there could not have been any current impressive development of special economic zones without the reform and opening up. The successful practice in the Shenzhen Special Economic Zone shows that economic development can also be rapidly promoted in order to achieve modernization under the socialist conditions. The tremendous historical achievements have been made in China's economic and social development in the past 30 years or more because our Party closely focused on the theme – development and resolutely pressed ahead with the reform and opening up. Comrade Deng Xiaoping once stated that the reform and opening up was a solution which determined China's fate, the principle behind this aspect should be sufficiently explained. General Secretary Hu Jintao also pointed out that the reform and opening up was a critical choice which determined the destiny of contemporary China; the reform and opening up accorded with the aspirations of the Party and the people, went along with the trend of the times, its direction and route were completely correct, and its effects and achievements cannot be denied, while there was no way out if standstill and retrogression had occurred. As indicated by the practice in Shenzhen's reform and opening up, first, the criteria for judging the success of reform and opening up are mainly as follows: It is beneficial for developing the productive forces of a socialist society, it is conducive to enhancing the comprehensive strength of a socialist country, and it is favorable for improving the people's living standing. Second, the reform and opening up require efforts in overcoming the "capitalist phobia". The successful experience of Shenzhen's practice is that we should not concentrate on abstractly debating the issue about whether or not we should follow the "socialist" or the "capitalist" road; instead, once we have a clear target, we should make bold attempts to achieve breakthroughs.

(III) The basic socialist economic system can be effectively combined with a market economy

In the final analysis, the practical success in the Shenzhen Special Economic Zone is the success in pushing forward with market-oriented reform. The Shenzhen Special Economic Zone fully utilized the reform and experimental power conferred on it by the Central Government, established a market-oriented reform mode from the beginning, and unswervingly moved forward in market-oriented reforms. According to the strategic intent of the Central Government for establishing special economic zones, people in the Shenzhen Special Economic Zone went beyond the existing system to make selections and comparisons among various target modes around the world, and combined the basic socialist economic system with the development of the market economy well; moreover, they promoted economic foundational change and that of superstructure change, and made Shenzhen become the first to carry out reform of the market-oriented economic system and the reform of the government's administrative management system, so as to gradually establish a relatively complete socialist market economy system and operational mechanism, and to acquire valuable experience for the reform of the national market economic system. Deng Xiaoping specially stressed that there was no fundamental contradiction between socialism and a market economy, the issue was that of which method should be adopted to develop social productive forces in a more vigorous way; the planned economy was not equal to socialism since there was also planning in a capitalist economy; a market economy was not equal to a capitalist one since there was also a market in socialism; both planning and market were economic means. Based on the exploration and practice of the reform of the market-oriented economic system in the Shenzhen Special Economic Zone, we can realize that: first, the socialist system should be combined with a market economy. Some foreigners believe that there is antinomy between socialism and a market economy, that both cannot coexist. The practical success of market-oriented reform in the special economic zones proves that the socialist system can be combined well with a market economy; second, a market economy is the only way for developing the economy. Unprecedentedly practicing a market economy rather than rigidly following the old road of the planned economy under the socialist conditions is the cause for successes in the special economic zones. The fact of rapid economic development in the special economic zones proves that though the market economic system is defective, it is really a vibrant economic system, an economic system which arouses the enthusiasm and creativity of workers. Only a market economy can provide a lasting driving force for rapid economic development and long-term prosperity.

(IV) We must persist in the reform and opening up, make reference to the shared achievements in human civilization

The opening up is a strong force in driving Shenzhen's development forward. There would be no flourishing Shenzhen today without the opening up. The Shenzhen Special Economic Zone was the first to attract a great deal of capital, technologies, talents and management experience through Sino-foreign joint ventures, Sino-foreign cooperation and wholly foreign-owned enterprises, etc. by utilizing the policies given by the Central Government, its location advantage in proximity to Hong Kong, actively making use of both domestic and international markets and two kinds of resources. First, it is essential for integrating into the world's economic system in order to pursue development. As a developing country, China cannot isolate itself from the process of economic globalization if the country strives to develop. China should actively expand its opening up to the outside world and vigorously participate in the international division of labor and cooperation so as to accelerate the construction of socialism with Chinese characteristics. As Comrade Deng Xiaoping mentioned, experience has proved that carrying out construction behind closed doors cannot bring about success, and China's development cannot do without integration into the world. Second, we should boldly absorb and draw upon all of civilization's achievements made throughout human society, including the useful results from capitalism. The preliminary effective combination of socialism with the most advanced things from developed capitalist countries and territories precisely boosts rapid economic development and overall social progress in Shenzhen. Third, there is no real reform without the opening up. The opening up is a major impetus for reform and also serves as an important means for reform. Promoting reform through the opening up is an important piece of experience gained from Shenzhen.

(V) Scientific development should be pursued and only concurrent improvement of both spiritual and material civilizations signifies real socialism

The Shenzhen Special Economic Zone has placed an equal emphasis on both spiritual and material civilizations, with active exploration of the new way for building a socialist spiritual civilization under the reform, the opening-up and market economy conditions, playing an exemplary role in promoting the all-round development of both spiritual and material civilizations. People in the Shenzhen Special Economic Zone have proceeded from actual conditions, put forward a new goal for building an efficient, harmonious Shenzhen and have clarified new thoughts and new measures for fostering "four-in-one" comprehensive, coordinated economic, political, cultural and social development. Shenzhen's practice presents the following several inspirations: first, the construction of material civilization is the foundation for building other civilizations, it is imperative for giving the first priority to development; second, the construction of material civilization, political civilization and ecological construction ultimately needs to be supported and motivated by the construction of spiritual civilization; third, coordinated development must be pursued in the construction of material civilization, political civilization, spiritual civilization and ecological civilization, while a severe lag in or less emphasis on any of these civilizations will affect the development of the overall society.

Progressive Advancement of China's Opening Up

Wang Zixian

Abstract In the 30-year reform and opening up—a new long march, China overcame all difficulties and obstacles to successfully achieve various historic missions for promoting development and reform through opening up and made remarkable achievements, becoming an important beneficiary of economic globalization. Practice proves that taking an open development path is the most important hallmark of the "China Model" and creates a successful case of leapfrog development in the world. China will conform to the new trend of economic globalization to push forward a new round of opening up in an all-round way and continuously break new ground in the opening up.

Keywords Opening up · Open development · Economic globalization

1 In the Past 30 Years, China Has Developed a Successful Mode of Open Development in the World

(I) The course of the opening up and its great achievements

In 1978, the Third Plenary Session of the 11th Central Committee of the Communist Party of China put forward the policy for China's opening up, followed by further establishing it as a basic policy. Afterwards, China's door was decidedly opened to the outside world. In almost 30 years, China scored tremendous achievements through its opening up, while China's opening up became an important driving force for China's construction modernization, thus helping

Wang Zixian (1963–2015), former Deputy Director, Policy Research Department of the Ministry of Commerce, Contract Research Fellow, PhD in Economics, University of International Business and Economics, research direction: international trade, macro economy, etc.

W. Zixian (✉)
Policy Research Department of the Ministry of Commerce,
University of International Business and Economics, Beijing 100731, China

Y. Yuan (ed.), *Studies on China's Special Economic Zones*, Research Series on the Chinese Dream and China's Development Path,
DOI 10.1007/978-981-10-3704-7_4

accumulate important experience in promoting construction modernization under the opening-up condition and vigorously pushing forward ideological emancipation and the transformation of concepts. Generally, China's opening up underwent the following three developmental stages: the first stage from 1978 to 1991 involved the experimentation of the opening up characterized by pilot work; the second stage from 1992 to 2000 featured policy-driven expansion of the opening up; the third stage from 2001 until now has been a stage of all-round opening up with institutional opening up as its characteristic. Marked by China's accession to the WTO, China's opening up switched from a stage dominated by local policy-based opening up to another stage mainly defined by comprehensive institutional opening up.

China's accession to the WTO has changed the historical course of China's economic development; China has moved to fully satisfy multilateral rules and external commitments, and has smoothly conformed to an international multilateral economic system, initiating the process of full integration into the world's economy. The largest externality of China's accession to the WTO is that China's full integration into the multilateral system has greatly changed the recognition and expectations of China's roles by the international community. China has really entered the stage of strategic cooperation with the international economy, especially a new stage of comprehensive upgrading of its strategic cooperation with multinational corporations, thus creating a successful mode of leapfrog development based on the opening up in the world especially in emerging countries. China's opening up first resulted in the rapid development of foreign trade. From 1978 to 2006, foreign trade soared by 84 times, making China the third largest trading nation in the world. Cumulative utilized foreign capital amounted to 685.5 billion USD, topping the list of developing countries. Annual turnover of foreign economic cooperation skyrocketed by 1189 times from 0.03 billion USD to 35.7 billion USD. A historic breakthrough was made in foreign investments—as of the end of 2006, the cumulative net amount of foreign direct investments reached 90.6 billion USD, and the amount of investments in 2006 ranked No. 13 in the world. In a horizontal comparison, China became the country with the fastest development of foreign trade in the world in this period.

The vigorous development of foreign trade also promoted the growth of the national economy and the expansion of employment. The role of foreign trade in stimulating the growth of a national economy has been on the rise. Currently, China's foreign-related taxes account for about 40% of total national taxes, and the number of people directly employed in the foreign trade field is nearly 0.1 billion, making up 1/3 of the national urban employment.

The opening up has substantially accelerated China's industrialization and modernization, enabling China to achieve leapfrog development. Rated as a new world factory by the circle of foreign critics, China has become an important manufacturing base in the world. The proportion of China's industrial added value in the world rose from 0.2% in 1980 to 8.2% in 2005, thus China ranked No. 3 in the world in this regard, only second to the USA and Japan. The opening up has introduced an awareness of the market economy and advanced management experience, giving a strong impetus to the establishment and improvement of the socialist market economy system. Thanks to the opening up, the proportions of both China's trade and economy in the world have dramatically increased, China's contributions to world trade and to economic development have significantly improved, and China's voice and influence in international economic affairs have been evidently enhanced. In 2006, China's foreign trade accounted for 8% of the world's foreign trade, while China's GDP made up 5% of that of the world and China's contributions to the growth of the world economy exceeded 11%. According to some research conducted by the World Bank, the degree of contribution to the world economy by China's economic growth from 2003 to 2005 ranked No. 2, only second to that of the USA.

(II) **China has created a successful model of open development worldwide**

As described in the Report of the 17th National Congress of the Communist Party of China, the door has been decisively opened to the outside world from coastal areas to the areas along rivers and borders, from eastern areas to central and western areas. Owing to this extensive unprecedented opening up, China has successfully achieved a great historical turnabout from a close, semi-closed country to a country open to the outside world in an all-round way. China's development path in the new period, especially its adherence to and expansion of the opening up, active integration in the global economy is hailed as the "Beijing Consensus" in the international economic circles, and such path has been fully recognized and highly commended worldwide. The "China Model" for taking the open developmental path has been acquired and imitated by developing countries. The tremendous achievements made in China through its opening up have been fully recognized by *Quand La Chine Change Le Monde (When China Changes the World)* (2005) written by French Erik Izraelewicz, *The World is Flat* (2006) written by American Thomas L Friedman, *The Next Global Stage* (2007) written by Japanese Kenichi Ohmae and other works, and international economic organizations including the World Bank, the World Trade Organization, the International Monetary Fund and the United Nations Conference on Trade and Development. China enjoys a higher degree of opening up than all of the other developing countries and believes more in globalization than many developed countries. All of the successes in China are marked by the reform and opening up, namely globalization. As described in the book entitled *Quand La Chine Change Le Monde*, Chinese leaders have integrated China's economy into the world market, jumpstarting China; in particular, China's accession to the WTO in 2001 fully broke the wall which isolated China from the outside world; China has become open to the outside world in a faster, wider and deeper way than other emerging economies.

China's takeoff occurred at the beginning of the new stage of globalization—in the last 20 years of the 20th century, when trade liberalization and the IT revolution led to the real outburst of world trade. When Japan and the Four Asian Tigers took off, world trade grew annually by only 5% on average; when China developed on a large scale, the annual growth rate of commodity trade in the world reached 10%. Furthermore, international capital and factor flow also fully accelerated during the new stage of globalization. Foreign investments in China were experimental in the 1980s; however, the stage of foreign strategic investments came as from 1992–1993. The cooperation between multinational corporations and China was further upgraded after China's accession to the WTO. At present, any large western corporation cannot be deemed as a large world-class corporation if it has no investments in China. In the past 20 years, multinational corporations invested 550 billion USD in China, a new world record. So far, none of the countries that are taking off in the region is fully open to foreign capital like China is. Being extraordinarily open-minded, Chinese leaders have the desire to take advantage of the globalization of the new stage to the fullest by utilizing foreign capital and introducing foreign advanced technologies, operational philosophies, managerial methods, high-end talents and marketing networks. Moreover, China has continuously improved its capability for self-dependent innovation through the opening up, and has become a new large research and development country. In its series on East Asian Studies, including Innovative East Asia—The Future of Growth, the World Bank has fully recognized China's successful practice in promoting innovations through its opening up.

(III) China's economic openness has markedly increased

First, the dependence on foreign trade continued to rise. The World Bank believed early that with efforts in more than ten years, China's dependence on foreign trade reached the average level of developing countries in the mid 1990s. Afterwards, such indicator constantly climbed. China's accession to the WTO drove a new round of rapid development of foreign trade. China's foreign trade grew annually by 28.3% on average from 2002 to 2006, up 18.3 percentage points compared with annual average GDP growth in the same period, while the dependence on foreign trade increased from 42.7% in 2002 to 67.0% in 2006 (Table 1).

Second, China has seized the historic opportunities in three international industrial transfers to successfully achieve the upgrading of an industrial structure,

Table 1 China's dependence on foreign trade in goods over the years (%)

Year	Dependence on foreign trade in goods	Dependence on exportation of goods	The proportion of industrial added value in the industrial product exporting industry
1985	22.7	8.9	11.5
1990	29.6	15.9	32.2
1995	38.6	20.4	43.0
2000	39.6	20.8	47.4
2001	38.5	20.1	46.6
2002	42.7	22.4	53.5
2003	51.9	26.7	62.3
2004	59.8	30.7	72.8
2005	63.3	33.9	80.9
2006	67.0	36.9	91.6

cultivate the comparative advantages and the competitive power in the whole industrial chain, and improve its status in the international division of labor.

Third, two-way cross-border flows of China's production factors have been comprehensively enhanced. The utilization of foreign capital is the most successful aspect of China's opening up and is an important motive power for continuously increasing China's openness. Currently, China has become the first choice for transnational investments and has ranked No. 1 among developing countries in attracting foreign investments for a long time. China has come out in front among various countries in the world in attracting FDI since the mid 1990s (Table 2). The absorption of foreign capital has filled the financing gap; more importantly, such absorption covered the severe shortage of endogenous capabilities and made up for the deficiencies in the whole production factor chain in China to boost China's capabilities in the whole industrial chain at the stage of China's economic takeoff and transition, thus China participated in the global optimal allocation of factors by starting from "introducing from foreign countries", smoothly started and subsequently promoted its economic internationalization at low costs and low risks. In China as a large country with a huge population, the proportion of foreign investments in China's GDP, investment and output value is not high compared with the international average level (Table 3), but from the perspective of the actual historical course of China's economic development, the roles of foreign investments are very prominent, and are embodied in not only the quantity, but also the quality, structure, talents, advanced management, advanced philosophy, institutional innovation, technical innovations, etc.

Fourth, China has become the world's factory and enjoys a very high level of internationalization in the manufacturing industry. Presently, China has deeply participated in the international division of labor from the low-end labor-intensive light textile industry to the high-end IT industry, and China has become an important link in the international industrial chain and has relatively high degrees of external dependence; for example, the degree of dependence on exports of garments, footwear and other goods is about 50%, while that of the emerging high-end products is higher.

Table 2 The proportion and ranking of foreign investments absorbed by China in the world

	1990	1995	1998	1999	2000	2001	2002	2003	2004	2005	2006
Amount of foreign direct investments (100 million USD)	34.9	375.2	454.6	403.2	407.2	468.8	527.4	535.1	606.3	603.3	694.7
The proportion in the world (%)	1.67	11.18	6.58	3.71	2.9	5.73	7.77	9.56	8.7	6.7	5.6
The ranking in the world	13	2	3	8	7	6	3	2	4	3	4

Source United Nations Conference on Trade and Development's World Investment Report 1995–2006

Table 3 The proportion of foreign direct investments absorbed by China in the national economy (%)

	1991	1995	1999	2000	2001	2002	2003	2004	2005	2006
The proportion in the GDP	1.1	5.2	3.7	3.4	3.5	3.6	3.3	3.1	2.7	2.7
The proportion in national fixed asset investments	4.2	15.7	11.2	10.3	10.5	10.1	8.0	7.2	5.6	5.0
The proportion of industrial added value from foreign-funded enterprises in national industrial added value			20.7	22.5	24.6	25.7	27.2	27.8	28.6	28.2

Source The Ministry of Commerce, National Bureau of Statistics

According to a survey released by the Organization for Security and Co-operation in Europe, the exportation of Chinese information and communication products amounted to 180 billion EUR in 2004, and as a result, China surpassed the USA to become the largest information and communication product exporting country in the world. A total number of 233 million mobile phones were made in China, among which 146 million mobile phones were exported, with the proportion of exports being 62.7%, and one out of three mobile phones among global exports came from China. In 2003, 210 million cameras were manufactured in China, among which 117.53 million ones were exported, accounting for 56.0%, including 61 million digital cameras, and more than one out of two digital cameras in global sales were made in China. They accounted for 53% of world trade. In 2004, Chinese notebook computers made up 40% of the world's total output, among which more than 25 million ones were exported, accounting for more than 70% of world trade. A total of 148 million DVDs were manufactured, among which 130 million ones were exported, accounting for 80% of world trade. Various kinds of displayers accounted for 50% of the world's total quantity. More than 170 kinds of products ranked No.1 in terms of export volume.

Fifth, the degree of China's market openness was fully increased, and systems and policies were geared to international standards after China's accession to the WTO. China has really become a conscious observer and maker of international economic rules under the conditions of globalization. The uncertain perceptions and expectations about China's economic internationalization by the international community have been completely changed, thus creating a new situation for China's opening up. In learning and assimilating foreign advanced technologies, management experience, operational philosophy, high-end talents, research, development and design, marketing networks, etc., China has developed a more open developmental thinking and philosophy. With its own efforts, China has firmly implemented the basic policy for opening up to take a successful path for the development of open industrialization and modernization.

Sixth, China has cooperated with various countries in the world in a mutually beneficially, win-win way, and has witnessed all-round improvement of its economic and trade relations. The most important example is that China has moved to an increasingly high place in ranking in the trade volume of its major trading partners and surrounding countries. China's import and export trade volume ranks No. 1 in the foreign trade of five economies (China is their largest trading partner), and is among the top three and six in the foreign trade of 28 and 64 economies, respectively. The trading partners of which China is the largest trading partner are concentrated in East Asia, including Chinese Hong Kong, Chinese Macau, South Korea, Chinese Taiwan and Mongolia, with trade volumes accounting for 45.8, 30.4, 18.6, 17.6 and 8.1% of the total trade volume, respectively. Currently, with respect to developed countries, China is among the top three trading partners of the USA, Canada, Japan, Australia and the EU, and ranks from the 4th–6th places in the foreign trade of the UK, the Netherlands, Luxembourg, Switzerland, Norway, Finland, Iceland, Israel, New Zealand, etc. The proportions of China's foreign trade in the total foreign trade of Japan, the USA, Australia and the EU exceed 10%, being 17.2, 11.9, 13.5 and 10.0%, respectively. In addition, China has also increasingly become an important trading partner of the world's continents. China ranks No. 1 in Asia's foreign trade, and has climbed to the second place in the EU's foreign trade. China ranks No. 3 in the foreign trade of Africa, the Commonwealth of the Independent States, Europe, No. 4 in the foreign trade of North America and Latin America, and No. 6 in the foreign trade of the Middle East.

2 The Opening Up Has Entered a New Stage

Marked by profound changes in China's domestic and international environment, China is entering a new historical stage of all-round, institutional opening up. Its main characteristic is that China will really enter an opening-up stage of full two-way cross-border flow of commodities and factors, at which there will be more striking requirements for coordinated development of commodity flow and factor flow, trade in goods and trade in services, imports and exports, absorption of foreign investments and investments in foreign countries, localization, internationalization, etc.

(I) The end of the transitional period after China's accession to the WTO and the improvement of China's per-capita income level are two large important hallmarks of entry into a new stage of the opening up

The end of the transitional period after China's accession to the WTO means that China is really approaching a new historical starting pointing for all-round institutional opening up. On the one hand, China shall fully observe the WTO's multilateral rules and conform to international standards to a higher degree, quicken the pace of integration into the global economy, participate intensely in economic globalization, and some protective measures and preferential policies reserved in the past in the transitional period have to be adjusted, and the WTO's principles of non-discrimination and national treatment must be more universally observed, and accelerating the transformation from policy-based opening up to all-round institutional opening up is an inevitable requirement after the transitional period. On the other hand, in view of the objective situation in which China undergoes a transformation towards a market economic system and internal, and external economic interactions become more intense during the new stage, we shall strive to achieve the goal of establishing a more mature open economic system; given that the opening up will become an intrinsic requirement for China's market economy system, it is necessary for speeding up the adjustment and innovation of the foreign economic system and relevant domestic policies. At the new stage, the opening-up policies fit for the overall market-oriented improvement of China's economic system will generally tend to be neutral, and these policies will be mainly based on internationally-accepted practices including the improvement of public services, administrative efficiency, the reduction of transaction costs, the promotion of trade and investment liberalization and facilitation, so as to serve the formation of new advantages for China's involvement in international economic cooperation and competition under the conditions of economic globalization, and the overall increase of its open economic level.

The excess of the level of China's per-capita income over 2000 USD is another important mark of the opening up at the new stage. Such a stage will witness the golden opportunities for China's opening up and a great variety of external contradictions. New situations and new problems will emerge. As stressed by Jiang Xiaojuan (2007), the following problems are specially salient: first, commodity exports will be subject to increasing barriers and restrictions at this stage; for example, when Japan's per-capita income reached 2204 USD in 1971, Japan faced a soaring trade surplus and foreign exchange reserve, huge pressure on domestic currency appreciation, excess liquidity, full escalation of trade frictions, a flare-up of contradictions in foreign relations, etc., which are very similar to the problems that we are confronting; second, China has also entered a stage at which the net inflow of international direct investments will decrease and the scale of indirect investments will surpass that of direct investments, which means that China will shift to a stage with full two-way cross-border flow of commodities and factors; finally, the opening up will increasingly become a macro issue—macro control is largely affected by both domestic and international factors, and the control exercised by the government over the domestic market tends to decline, and the space for China's policy choice diminishes Therefore, at the new stage, the opening up is a strategic issue concerning the overall national economic and social development and a focal point which attracts attention from the international community rather than an issue relating to a certain field.

(II) Accelerated extension of economic globalization from the manufacturing industry to the service industry is a major international background for the opening up during the new stage

As the new century begins, economic globalization has been continuously advancing in depth and breadth; subsequently, optimal global allocation of resources by the people has reached an unprecedented level; in particular, the IT revolution has made a "global village" come true to a large extent; the world has become smaller and flatter. At present, a new round of reorganization of international production factor and industrial transfer is on the rise. A new large background for China's opening up is that service globalization is surging along with the transformation of the world economy towards a service economy. The modernization and globalization of the service industry is exerting a significant far-reaching impact on the economy in countries around the world, while its level is the key to determining the statuses of countries in the international industrial chain, innovation chain and value chain.

Presently, the globalization of the service industry presents a series of new trends—multinational corporations in developed countries are speeding up their transformation towards service-oriented enterprises and have become the main body for driving the globalization of the service industry; moreover, they are leveraging core advantages in research, development and marketing and in other fields to occupy the commanding height for international competition. The globalization of the service industry is also manifested as follows: two-way trade and investments in the service industry are rapidly growing, and the transnational transfer of the service industry is dominating a new round of international industrial transfers; international service outsourcing is the latest mark of the globalization of the service industry; in its latest report, the World Bank calls it the "global outsourcing of the service industry". Though international service outsourcing started late, it is growing at an astonishing rate. According to the latest research conducted by BearingPoint, the scale of the global service outsourcing industry was 917.8 billion USD in 2006, among which IT service outsourcing and business process accounted for 54 and 46%, respectively. It is expected that, in the future, the international service outsourcing industry will be further widened, become more diverse in modes, and will play a bigger role in reducing costs, promoting world trade, investment and the world's economic integration. China will meet the historical opportunities for undertaking the transfer and outsourcing of the international service industry to accelerate modernization and will also face unprecedented challenges.

(III) As China has entered a new period of construction modernization, it is necessary to further expand the opening up

For the new stage, China has ushered in a crucial period of building an affluent society in an all-around way—a period beneficial for golden development but fraught with contradictions. China's tasks for sustainable development will be more arduous, and domestic employment, resource and environmental pressure will be more obvious; it is urgent for us to further open wider to the outside world, increase the level of utilization of both markets and both resources—both domestic and foreign markets, both domestic and foreign resources.

First, national conditions and characteristics require more sufficient use of both resources and both markets. China is always subject to the contradiction between the increasing material and cultural needs of the people and the backward social production, thus it is essential for absorbing all human civilization achievements through the opening up to expedite modernization. One outstanding characteristic of China's national conditions is that the factor structure is imbalanced and various factors are unmatched in China. As the economic internationalization is promoted, we can more fully utilize external resources, factors and markets, and our factor allocation and production structure can be free from the severe constraints of natural endowments.

Second, expanding the opening up is an inevitable requirement for quickening the transformation of the economic developmental model. Practice proves that under the conditions of economic globalization, taking an open development path is conducive to improving the efficiency of resource allocation and enhancing the competitive power. China is one of the countries which actively participate in and most benefit from economic globalization. In order to accelerate the transformation of the economic developmental model, improve the quality of economic development and quicken modernization in the future, China must further expand its opening up, adapt to the new trend of economic globalization and increase its level of participation in economic globalization.

Third, expanding its opening up is beneficial to pushing forward mutually beneficial, win-win economic and trade relations. On the one hand, with the expansion of its opening up, China will provide more market access, economic and trade cooperation opportunities for countries around the world, and mutually beneficial cooperation with various countries will be generally further boosted; on the other hand, though the conflict of interests and competition between China and some countries are on the rise, only further intensifying economic and trade exchanges, especially increasing interest complementation and convergence, can contradictions and frictions be resolved.

3 A New Round of Opening Up Is Promoted in an All-Round Way

In the new historical period, the international competition for China will become fierce, and external pressure will exist for a long time; furthermore, there are more and more risks which can be predicted and others that are hardly predictable. We should gain a deep understanding of new issues and new contradictions for China's development, and comprehensively press ahead with a new round of opening up to continue becoming an important beneficiary of economic globalization in the new period, so as to make more contributions to achieving a great rejuvenation of the Chinese nation and promoting the building of a harmonious world.

(I) Further widen the channels for the opening up, actively and orderly carry forward multi-tier opening up

First, as a large economic and trade country, China should carry out a long-term strategy for actively boosting the building of a more open global trade and investment mechanism. This is our need for safeguarding our long-term interests. We should proceed from the overall situation and a long-term perspective to more proactively participate in multilateral negotiations, utilize multilateral rules to balance the interests of various parties, and safeguard and promote a global free trade and investment system. We should broaden communication and cooperation, and impel interest convergence for jointly coping with global economic and social difficulties.

Second, China should further propel a regional, multilateral opening up. China should earnestly implement a free trade zone strategy, actively take part in regional economic cooperation at various levels, and focus on East Asian regional economic cooperation to foster a pattern of all-around regional economic cooperation. Based on bilateral economic and trade cooperation, China should continue to fully enhance economic and trade cooperation with developing countries and tap emerging markets while consolidating economic and trade relations with developed countries.

Third, we should keep on drawing upon the past successful experience and persevere in an active opening up. As China sees a significant improvement in industrial competitiveness and labor productivity, China enjoys a potential for further opening up the market; given the possibilities and needs of the development of a national economy and industry, we should actively push ahead with our opening up in various fields and different regions to better serve the general situation of China's modernization.

(II) Expand the regional opening up, continue serving as the model forerunner as a special economic function zone

According to empirical research conducted by many authoritative experts, the main players in today's economic globalization are not merely national countries, but companies, individuals, consumers and vibrant regions have constituted an increasingly important principal part in economic globalization. As obviously indicated by the practice in emerging countries, including India and many developed economies, some of their important regions and central cities have become the most dynamic forerunners in their economy, and have first made innovations to achieve a great leap forward in development and have acted as its important models, radiators and drivers. In the past, China's Pearl River Delta and Yangtze River Delta were the successful models for implementing the developmental strategy driven by the opening up in the manufacturing industry, while at the present, central cities including Dalian have become the forerunners in undertaking international service transfer and outsourcing, etc. In the future, as China will still undergo institutional transition, there will be an important strategic significance for giving full play to the roles of China's important regions and central cities as pacesetters and models in economic internationalization. Regarding this aspect, China will make new strategic forward-looking experimentations by shaping a new situation of economic internationalization and better promoting coordinated regional economic development. First, coastal areas of eastern China will continue serving as the forerunners in accommodating the international high-end manufacturing industry and the modern service industry, especially in carrying out advanced reforms and institutional innovations in the service industry, thus accelerating its transformation towards the service economy; second, central cities, in the central and western regions, where conditions permit, will be built into open platforms for undertaking international and eastern industrial transfer, forming the largest open belt covering the east-west, north-south hinterland; third, intensified efforts will be made to build the mechanism of regional cooperation with adjacent countries, as an important breakthrough, to improve the opening-up of border areas, boost the development and opening-up of the northeast old industrial base, and foster new open belts and growth poles; fourth, in line with the general situation of the development of the special economic function zones worldwide, actions will be taken to speed up the transformation of China's special function zones, where conditions permit, including special economic zones, economic and technological developmental zones towards standardized free trade zones, especially build service-oriented free trade zones, create new advantages for China to participate in service globalization and realize a great leap forward in the development of the service industry.

(III) Add more fields for opening up, give priority to the service industry in the new round of opening up

We should keep expanding the fields for opening up and generate a wide-ranging opening-up pattern. It is necessary to focus on the service industry in the new round of opening up while enlarging the opening up in the manufacturing, agricultural and social fields. We should make reference to the successful experience in the open development of the manufacturing industry, energetically participate in the globalization of the service industry, and carry out the important strategic measure—making the service industry more open to the outside world—and actively undertake the international service outsourcing—to accelerate the development and upgrading of the service industry, so as to bring about a great leap forward in the development of the service industry and speed up China's modernization. It is essential to adapt to the new situations of informatization, modernization and globalization of the world's service industry, endeavoring to introduce more from foreign countries to the service industry for expediting the reform and reorganization of China's service industry. We should also lose no time in initiating the process of globalizing the service industry to advance in foreign countries with the resources of others. We should undertake international service outsourcing, a breakthrough made for China to participate in the globalization of the service industry and expand the opening-up of the service industry.

We should sharpen the competitive edge in absorbing the international transfer of the service industry, and promote development, reforms and innovations through the opening up. We should accelerate institutional innovations and optimize public services to create better conditions for the enterprises in the service industry to participate in international cooperation and competition amidst violent storms and waves. We should speed up the reorganization, reform and reconstruction of the service industry, introduce an advanced management system, operational philosophy, software and hardware technologies and new business types from foreign service providers to enhance the innovation capability of the service industry and quicken the modernization of this industry.

(IV) Stimulate the two-way cross-border flow of production factors, increase investments in foreign countries

We should follow the new trend of economic globalization by actively promoting the two-way flow of production factors, enable coordinated development of going global and introducing from foreign countries, improve the optimal allocation of resources worldwide, form new advantages for participating in international competition and cooperation amid globalization. On the one hand, we should still actively, effectively utilize foreign capital, enhance the quality of foreign capital absorption to make it an important way for promoting self-dependent innovations; on the other hand, as another key point for the new round of opening up, we should increase investments in foreign countries and raise the international operation level of Chinese enterprises. First, we should carry forward continued innovations of the institutional and reform environment for investments in foreign countries; we should better support the international operation of enterprises in research, development, production and sales etc., and help them quicken the pace of going global; second, we should draw upon the experience from developed countries, speed up the formation of the promotion system for overseas investment service led by commercial banks; third, we should build a number of multinational corporations and international famous brands; fourth, we should vigorously support the international operation of small and medium-sized enterprises, increase support, especially improve policy-based financial support.

(V) Further strengthen international cooperation in the energy resource field

China is a country with a relative shortage of resources. Per-capita quantities of oil and natural gas in China are lower than 1/8 and 1/20 of those in the world respectively. Per-capita proven reserves of 45 major non-ferrous metal resources in China are only half of the world's average level. The contradictions in the supply of some important bulk energy resources have been sharpening and the dependence on the international market has become more profound since the new round of economic growth began. In the future, with industrialization, urbanization, especially the expansion of the heavy chemical industry, the contradictions regarding energy resources may continue and worsen for a considerable length of time. Currently, China's utilization of overseas resources mainly relies on spot trade, while the proportion of the development of investments and equity resources is obviously low, thus there is an urgent need for intensifying the cooperative development of overseas resources. It is essential to continue supporting large state-owned enterprises in establishing overseas energy resource bases and guiding various types of private enterprises to systematically engage in the cooperative development of overseas resources. Meanwhile, we should actively participate in cooperation and coordination in the international energy resource field, strengthen our resource-related diplomatic work, and develop the necessary fiscal, tax and financial support policies more rapidly.

(VI) **Promote joint development in a mutually beneficial, win-win way**

China's development cannot be isolated from the world, while the world's prosperity also needs China. China always steadfastly implements the opening up strategy for mutual benefits and win-win results. China advocates economic cooperation and advantage complementation to jointly promote the balanced, universally beneficial and win-win development of economic globalization. China works with the people from various countries to build a harmonious world with lasting peace and prosperity for all. China continues to advance regional and global joint development through its development. First, China expands its interest convergence with various parties, considers the right concerns of its economic and trading partners, especially developing countries, and safeguards the legitimate rights and interests of partners; second, China properly addresses conflicts of interest and competition by reinforcing complementation and cooperation, and appropriately deals with economic and trade frictions through communication and consultation; third, China supports the international community in helping developing countries enhance their independent developmental capabilities, improve people's livelihood and narrow the north-south gap. Overall, China should enter into mutually beneficial, win-win economic and trading cooperation relations with countries around the world by expanding its opening up.

Shenzhen's Economy in the Context of China's Changing Growth Model

Vladimir Portyakov

Abstract The adjustments being made in China's economic growth model have national, regional, and local dimensions for the progress, specifics, and results of the adjustments made in the economic growth model to be followed and analyzed by the central government on the scale of the country's economy in general and in particular regions. In this context, the experience of economic development of Shenzhen in recent years is of considerable interest. From 2011 to 2013, Shenzhen's economy developed under constraints, the most painful of which were brought about by the worsening world market and growing labor costs in China. These circumstances forced the municipal authorities to start looking for hidden internal forces to drive the economy on. As a result, Shenzhen's economic growth and the economic growth model implemented on the ground in the city between 2011 and 2013 look similar to the developments and trends recognizable across China and, in a way, are different. The author follows the significant developmental trends in manufacturing and services in Shenzhen over the last few years.

Keywords China · Shenzhen · Economic growth model · Manufacturing · Services · Major trends

1 Introduction

The modification of China's economic growth model announced by the country's leadership and pursued, in varying measures, on the ground, has a national and regional or local dimension for the central government to monitor and analyze its progress, specificities, and returns on the scale of the national economy in general, and, provided that enough data are available, on the scale of individual regions. The two-track analysis helps the monitoring agency to spot innovative initiatives displayed at the grassroots in economic growth rates or structures that can be borrowed

V. Portyakov (✉)
RAS Institute for Far Eastern Studies, Moscow, Russia
e-mail: portyakov@ifes-ras.ru

Y. Yuan (ed.), *Studies on China's Special Economic Zones*, Research Series on the Chinese Dream and China's Development Path,
DOI 10.1007/978-981-10-3704-7_5

for application across a greater part of China. It may also be assumed that the regions' practices may, on close monitoring, probably contain elements likely to have an adverse corrective effect on general approaches to the modifications of the economic growth model in China.

In this context, the experience gained in the economic performance in Shenzhen in recent years deserves a closer scrutiny for several reasons. First, the Shenzhen special economic zone (SEZ), expanded on July 10, 2010 to cover the entire city, has been a leading experimental ground in the country for three decades for trying out numerous innovative approaches in foreign trade, administration, and many areas of reforms in the economy and social services. Second, the city has a very large and structurally diversified economy that gives weight to the ongoing search for innovations in various industries and makes it fully representative. A further important consideration is that while Shenzhen is ranked fourth among China's cities in gross regional product (GRP), it is first in GDP per capita (nearly $22,000), a strong enough reason for Shenzhen's performance to be rated as a singular experience. Third, it was a "we-had-it-before" experience for Shenzhen, a city that had been forced by circumstances to abruptly change tack in its leading economic role several times over its short history—at the midpoint of the last decade, its authorities first gave practical thought to overhauling the existing economic growth model, with its heavy reliance upon investments and exports. More specifically, they realized the significance of growth factors other than investments, consumption, and exports in stimulating growth in Shenzhen's GRP and encouraging the city to diversify its growth sources by, above all, raising the contribution of science and engineering and gradually lowering investments, demand, and export risks.[1]

2 The Characteristics of Shenzhen's Economic Development

Shenzhen's current economic growth benchmarks were largely set out in its five-year socio-economic developmental plan for the years 2011–2015 that was approved at the Second Session of the city's Fifth Assembly of the People's Representatives held between January 15 and 19, 2011. The plan called for an increase in Shenzhen's GRP to 1.5 trillion yuan (from 958 billion yuan in 2010) at an average annual growth of 10%, a rise of GDP per capita to $20,000 (from $14,600 in 2010), and an increase of 60% in the contribution of science and engineering to economic growth by the end of the five-year period. The share of

[1]Xin Hua, an expert in the management of the economy, who did research in Shenzhen, estimated that the aggregate investments, consumption, and exports were quite significant in the city in the early 1990s, peaking in 1992. In the period from 2001 to 2004, their contribution to the GRP leveled out at between 40 and 50%. Xin Hua, "The Resource Balance, Bearing Props, and Beneficiation of Production. A Study of Trends in the Future Development of Shenzhen and the Zhu Jiang Delta," Beijing, 2010, Foreword, pp. 53–54 [*in Chinese*].

advanced industries (biotechnology and Internet economics, among others) was to be raised to 20%, and that of services, to 60%.[2]

Between 2011 and 2013, Shenzhen's economy faced many adversities, including the most painful of them, a downturn of the world's economy that bit into foreign markets, and also the pressure building up on exports and the producers' and exporters' rising operating expenses. The coincidence of tighter foreign markets, climbing inflation, and rising labor costs in China cut into the profits of the manufacturing industries in Shenzhen as a whole.[3] A further inconvenience, the deadline passed for the income tax on enterprises in special economic zones and in the country in general to be leveled out and some of the city-based companies had their previous tax references retracted.[4]

The emerging situation pushed the municipal authorities to look around for internal (*neisheng*) forces to sustain the economic growth.[5]

Their efforts succeeded in advancing Shenzhen's economic growth to a level and making the economic growth model implemented, in practical terms, in the city, similar to the mainstream developments and trends typical of China in general, and still unparalleled anywhere in the country (see Table 1).

Unlike it is in the country as a whole, where the GDP has been slipping over the last three years (9.3, 7.8, and 7.7%, respectively), the GRP growth rate in Shenzhen has held at 10%, or higher. Over the time period covered here, investments in public fixed assets in Shenzhen followed an uptrend, at a much lower rate, though, than they were and are on the countrywide scale—between 2011 and 2013, investments grew at 23.6, 20.3, and 19.6%, respectively, on the national scale.[6] General retail trade in Shenzhen followed the national uptrend pattern at nearly the same countrywide rate that was 17.1% in 2011, 14.3% in 2012, and 13.1% in 2013.

Foreign trade has a special significance for Shenzhen, and it leads all other cities in China in annual count. In 2012, for example, Shenzhen made 12.9% of the national foreign trade averages, of which 13.8% was in exports and 11.9% in imports[7] for its 2.55% share of the country's GDP in 2013. Significantly, Shenzhen's foreign trade in recent years has been growing at a more even rate than

---

[2]http://sz.people.com.cn/GB/13746988.html. Retrieved on February 6, 2011.

[3]*See*: Report on the Economic Development of Shenzhen 2012 [*in Chinese*], Beijing, 2012, Foreword, p. 1.

[4]On January 1, 2008, a standardized income tax rate of 25% was imposed on all enterprises in China. Enterprises in the Shenzhen SEZ that had paid income tax at a preferential rate of 15% were now to pay it incrementally at 2–3% points every year, 18% through 2008, 20% in 2009, 22% in 2010, 24% in 2011, and 25% in 2012 and on. Enterprises that had a high export quota (70% or more) and manufactured high-tech products retained their tax benefits. Xin Hua, *Op. cit.*, p. 87.

[5]Report on the Economic Development of Shenzhen 2012, Foreword, p. 1.

[6]China Statistics in Brief 2012 [*in Chinese*], Beijing, 2012, p. 50; China Statistics in Brief 2013 [*in Chinese*], Beijing, 2013, p. 50; http://sz.people.com.cn/n/2014/10120/c202846-20431058.html.

[7]http://sz.people.com.cn/n/2014/0211/c262846-20540431.html.

Table 1 Economic growth in Shenzhen in 2011–2013

Item	Unit	2011	2012	2013
Gross regional product	Billions of yuan	1150.21	1295.01	1450.02
Growth	%	10.0	10.0	10.5
Value added in manufacturing	Billions of yuan	–	509.1	569.5
Growth	%	12.6	7.3	9.6
Investments in fixed assets	Billions of yuan	213.6	231.4	250.1
Growth	%	10.1	12.3	14.0
Retail sales	Billions of yuan	352.09	400.88	443.36
Growth	%	17.8	16.5	10.6
Foreign trade	$ bn	414.10	466.78	537.36
Growth	%	19.4	12.7	15.1
Exports	$ bn	245.53	271.37	305.72
Growth	%	20.2	10.5	12.7
Imports	$ bn	168.57	195.41	231.64
Growth	%	18.2	15.9	18.5

Sources Report on Economic Development in Shenzhen 2012 [*in Chinese*], Beijing, 2012, pp. 2–5; http://www.szrd.gov.cn/contenthtml/11/20140117100l6.html; and http://sz.people.com.cn/n/2014/0211/c262846-20540431.html

China's average −19.4, 12.7, and 15.1% for Shenzhen and 22.5, 6.2, and 7.6% for China generally.

The impression is, though, that the relative significance of foreign direct investments and the presence of a large group of partly foreign-owned enterprises, both major growth factors of Shenzhen's economic affluence, has been waning, if only a little, in recent years. With a huge amount of foreign direct investments it had drawn in over the years (in late 2011, $54.5 billion had actually been used up), Shenzhen still attracts much foreign funding, but it slid to approximately tenth place among China's cities in annual averages ($4.6 billion in 2011).[8] Besides, it so happens now and then, under the growing pressure of the world's economy, that enterprises and companies owned in part by foreign interests put in a worse performance than enterprises fully owned by Chinese investors. In 2011, to give an example, the added value rose by 3.3% from the year before for enterprises partly owned by foreign investors in China (including Hong Kong and Macau), which compares badly with the 12.6% for the added value growth in manufacturing nationwide.[9]

As we said above, Shenzhen has been forced to cast around for further internal growth-driving forces, and is doing this persistently in several directions simultaneously.

[8]Report on the Economic Development of Shenzhen 2012, pp. 35 and 13.

[9]Ibid., p. 3.

The city pays great attention to reducing the costs of energy and other primary resource inputs per unit of output. For example, primary energy inputs that went into production for the amount of 10,000 yuan of the GRP came out at the equivalent of 0.432 tons of fuel, or 4.3% less than they were in 2012, and the inputs of electric power worked out at 558.4 kWh, or 7.14% below the 2012 level.[10] Water inputs are going down, too.

The development of successful energy and resource saving technologies is closely related, directly and inversely, to the priority given in Shenzhen to research and development projects. The share of R&D outlays in the city's GRP climbed from 3.5% in 2010 to 3.81% in 2012[11] (it reached 1.98% in 2013 nationwide).

3 The Structural Change of Shenzhen's Economy

The structure of Shenzhen's economy differs significantly from that of the national economy.

The 2013 gross domestic product originated in the three groups of industries in the following proportions: 10.0% in Group I, 43.9% in Group II, and 46.1% in Group III.[12] The first group (primary industries) has virtually ceased to play any significant role in Shenzhen in the last few years, accounting for 0.1% of the city's GRP in 2010, and the added value of 525 million yuan generated in this group in 2013 contributed 0.036% to the GRP and was dropped out of aggregate statistics altogether. The share of the second group (secondary industries) fell from 47.2% in 2010 to 43.4% of GRP in 2013, while the share of the services (tertiary industries) rose from 52.7 to 56.6% of the GRP over the same period.[13]

Still, manufacturing that takes up a major part of Group II remains a key activity in Shenzhen, giving an overall direction and setting the main trends for adjusting the local model of economic growth. It is hard, though, to make any sense of what exactly sets manufacturing apart in Shenzhen or what changes have occurred in it in recent years because of the vague dividing lines drawn in general information and statistics on three manufacturing types—mainstay industries, new strategic industries, and high-tech industries. A single product type is often listed in all three groups, and it is difficult to eliminate overlaps from statistics, or avoid double counting. This is not an impediment, though, to getting an impartial picture of manufacturing in Shenzhen today. A hierarchy of mainstay manufacturing industries is shown in Table 2.

[10]http://sz.people.com.cn/n/2014/0211/c202846-20540431.html.

[11]http://szrd.gov.cn/contenthtml/11/2014011710016.html.

[12]*Calculated from:* http://sz.people.com.cn/n/2014/10120/c202846-20431058.html.

[13]Report on the Economic Development of Shenzhen 2012, p. 12.

Table 2 Mainstay manufacturing industries in Shenzhen according to annual added value

Name of industry	2009		2011	
	Billions of yuan	Share, %	Billions of yuan	Share, %
Electronics and communication equipment	172.12	50.18	282.08	54.0
Mechanical engineering	55.61	16.21	82.59	15.8
Oil production	27.72	8.08	42.03	8.0
Electric power supply	20.1	5.86	28.11	5.4
Plastics	9.69	2.83	11.60	2.2
Textiles	7.14	2.08	12.01	2.3
Printing and packaging	6.72	1.96		
Gold and precious metal articles	6.06	1.72	8.32	1.6
Articles from minerals, except for metal-containing minerals	3.67	1.07	5.39	1.0
Medical preparations	3.65	1.06	4.91	0.9
Chemical products			4.72	0.9
Total for all ten industries	312.50	91.1	481.77	92.1

Sources Report on the Economic Development of Shenzhen 2010 [*in Chinese*], Beijing, 2010, p. 21; Report on the Economic Development of Shenzhen 2012 [*in Chinese*], pp. 29–30

Manufacture of every kind of electronic equipment and components, with a 20% annual growth in added value in 2010 and 2011, is certainly the undisputed leader. In 2013, the industry's output rose to 316 billion yuan, up 12.8% compared to 2012.[14] Mechanical engineering comes next, and then, in third place, the offshore oil production on the continental shelf. Over recent years, the share of Shenzhen's manufactured products sold on the domestic market grew from 43.8% in 2010 to 46.6% in 2011.[15]

In the past few years, though, priority has been given to six new strategic industries. In 2013, they contributed 34.5% to Shenzhen's GRP, with a total added value of 500 billion yuan. These industries include biotechnologies (22.8 billion yuan in added value), the Internet economy (59 billion yuan), new energy sources (33.6 billion yuan), new materials (31 billion yuan), new-generation information equipment (218 billion yuan), and "innovative cultural products" (135.7 billion yuan).[16]

The "Innovative cultural products" industry has been developing in Shenzhen for over a decade now. The city leads the way in several types of this industry in China. In particular, it is home to over 200 industrial design companies, 49% of China's total, that control 60% of the domestic market in that industry.

---

[14]http://sz.people.com.cn/n/2014/0211/c202846-20540431.html.

[15]Report on the Economic Development of Shenzhen 2012, p. 31.

[16]http://sz.people.com.cn/n/2014/0211/c202846-20540431.html.

In late 2010, Shenzhen had 2467 print shops, making it the national center for producing high-quality printed matter.[17] Revenues from numerous subject parks take up a large share of the "innovative cultural products" structure.

Shenzhen's accent on promoting high-tech industries is among its obvious advantages. Their output rose more than tenfold over the first decade of the 21st century in value terms, from 106.4 billion yuan in 2000 to almost 1200 billion yuan in 2011. An important point to make, the city's high-tech sector, as a whole, kept up its positive growth even at the peak of the world economic crisis in 2009, and stepped it up significantly in the years following the crisis (see Table 3).

Development and export of the city's high-tech products fall back largely on its own R&D projects. By different estimates, between 40 and 60% of the total output are developed in Shenzhen. The state encourages and rewards the development and promotion of high-tech products. Since 2008, for example, the enterprises set up in Shenzhen (and in other special economic zones) manufacturing new and high-tech products have been exempted from income tax for two years from their startup. In the following three years, they were charged at a tax rate half the normal 25% income tax.[18]

By all appearances, a model innovative developmental cluster has shaped up in Shenzhen where borrowed and rewardingly bankrolled domestic scientific and engineering innovations can be launched into quantity production within very short time frames with support from the powerful and diversified high-tech industry. Another circumstance to note is that the central and local authorities help some new types of output to win their market niches. For example, an electric car by the BYD (Biyadi) company selling for 360,000 yuan gets a subsidy of 60,000 yuan from a government agency and another 60,000 yuan from Shenzhen authorities. This subsidized promotion policy doubled the electric car production in Shenzhen every year between 2009 and 2012 and made it a leader in low-carbon economy growth among the country's cities.[19]

Shenzhen's advanced economy—by national and, to an extent, international standards—shows up distinctly in the large proportion of services. Characteristically, services have not arisen in Shenzhen as a thing-in-itself; rather, they are a spinoff of the modern manufacturing and foreign trade facilities in the city that facilitates their advance.

Today, Shenzhen has four major categories of production-related services.[20]

First, there is a comprehensive system of modern open financial services provided by banks, a stock exchange, and insurance companies. The Shenzhen Development Bank has offices in provincial centers across China. The Shenzhen

[17]Report on the Economic Development of Shenzhen 2012, pp. 78–81. It is indicative, in a way, that the illustrated *Fenghuang* (Phoenix) magazine is published and circulated widely in Shenzhen, of all places.

[18]Xin Hua, *Op. cit.*, p. 87.

[19]*Renmin ribao*, April 1, 2013.

[20]Xin Hua, *Op. cit.*, p. 85.

Table 3 Manufacture of high-tech products in shenzhen

Product name	2009		2011	
	Output, billions of yuan	Growth, %	Output, billions of yuan	Growth, %
High-tech products, total	850.78	3.6	1187.56	16.7
Electronics and communication equipment	753.8	2.0	1,045.11	16.6
New materials and equipment for producing new kinds of energy	44.63	12.6	65.09	17.5
Combined opto-electro-mechanical products	38.65	18.4	57.46	17.1
Biotechnological and medical products	8.0	35.1	11.99	18.5
Environmental protection products	5.69	42.4	7.91	17.9
Export of high-tech products, billions of U.S. dollars	85.05	-5.5	124.8	14.8

Sources Report on the Economic Development of Shenzhen 2010 [*in Chinese*], Beijing, 2010, pp. 22–23; Report on the Economic Development of Shenzhen 2012 [*in Chinese*], pp. 31–32 and 34

Stock Exchange trades in shares of stock and is one of the two stock exchanges of its type in the country (aside from the stock exchange in Shanghai, yet another stock exchange operates in China's Hong Kong Special Administrative Region). The Shenzhen Stock Exchange has a floor for trading in stocks issued by innovative enterprises and another floor for trading in stocks of small and medium businesses. In mid-2013, trades made in stocks of innovative enterprises were valued at approximately a quarter of all trades conducted in stocks at the Shenzhen Stock Exchange.[21]

Second, there is a well-developed modern logistical system comprising the seaport and airport (a new airport has been in operation since late 2013), three duty-free customs zones (Futian, Shatuojiao, and Yantian), two export processing zones, one duty-free port zone, and over 60 duty-free warehouses and customs export bonded warehouses.[22] The Shenzhen seaport is fourth in the world for containerized goods transshipments (23 million ISO containers in 2013).

Third, a modern Internet-based information support and modern communication system.

Fourth, a system for implementing scientific and engineering ideas. Shenzhen has hosted a fair of new and high technologies since 1999.

Generally, modern services contribute over two-thirds of the income from the sale of services in Shenzhen (68% in 2012).[23]

[21]On July 22, 2013, a 25.84 billion yuan worth of stocks of innovative enterprises was traded in Shenzhen, where a total of 96.55 billion yuan (approximately $15 billion) in stocks was traded on the same day. http://sz.people.com.cn/n/2013/0722/c202846-19124944 1.html.

[22]Report on the Economic Development of Shenzhen 2012, p. 129.

[23]http://szrd.gov.cn/contenthtml/11/20140117l0016.html.

4 Conclusion

An analysis of the specific sectors of Shenzhen's economy over the last four to five years shows that the adjustments made in the economic growth model on the national scale are projected onto the regional level, above all as changes in the structure of manufacturing and services. It is not easy, though, to raise the role of consumption as an economic growth factor in Shenzhen, and all of China, for that matter. A major reason for this setback is, for the most part, that a significant proportion of the city's population come from other regions of the country and many of the new settlers remit a large proportion of their wages back home. Besides, Shenzhen residents satisfy some of their consumer needs in neighboring Hong Kong.

Some feedback that Shenzhen's practical ways may have on the modification of the country's general economic growth model is the city's successful attempt to switch many medium and small enterprises that have, for most of their history, processed customers' materials into products, from customer designs over to the manufacturing of more advanced products, and, from the strategic perspective, introduction of new and environment-friendly technologies within short time frames in Shenzhen. The city seems set to identify and develop its comparative advantages in full measure.

The approaches used in Shenzhen to promote modern manufacturing and services has deserved close attention from Russian experts and government agencies because the "Shenzhen model" is a textbook example of development that does not rely on raw materials, the need for which is felt keener in Russia today than at any time in the past.

A Study of Special Economic Zone Transformation and the China Model

Luo Qinghe, Wang Fang, Zhang Zhenfeng and Ke Xiao

Abstract The background of the "altruistic" establishment of China's traditional special economic zones determines that the special zones serve as "windows", "experimental fields", models and drivers, and they take up the historical mission of reducing the risks and costs of the national reform and opening up while paving the way for it. When the market-oriented reform of the special zones becomes the goal for national reforms, the traditional historical mission of the special economic zones will have basically been accomplished. This shows that the special zones have no longer mainly functioned as the windows for the opening up and the experimental fields for institutional reforms; instead, they have developed into a regional developmental model and have constituted a pole for the economic growth of this region. New special zones were established and special policies relating to them were set up to further aggregate the factors, promote the economic development of the new special zones, give rise to polarization and produce diffusion effects, which has become a new regional developmental model. The economic reform was mainly driven and put into practice by the special economic zones, thus the special zone mode developed by the traditional special zones and the new special zone developmental path is the foundation and core of the China Model.

Keywords Special economic zones · Transformation · Special zone mode · China model

The Third Plenary Session of the 11th Central Committee of the Communist Party of China established the basic policy for reform and the opening up to initiate the course of the great rejuvenation of the Chinese nation. In 35 years, China made a breakthrough—setting up the special economic zones—and continuously intensified the reforms, expanded the opening up to make tremendous achievements, gradually build a firm confidence in the socialist road with Chinese characteristics, theories and systems. In this process, the special economic zones grew from

L. Qinghe (✉) · W. Fang · Z. Zhenfeng · K. Xiao
College of Economics, Shenzhen University, Shenzhen 518060, Guangdong, China

Y. Yuan (ed.), *Studies on China's Special Economic Zones*, Research Series on the Chinese Dream and China's Development Path,
DOI 10.1007/978-981-10-3704-7_6

"windows" and "experimental fields" for reform and the opening up into a regional developmental model and then the foundation and core of the China Model.

1 Review of the Developmental History of Special Economic Zones Around the World

The special economic zones[1] have existed in the world for nearly five centuries, since Italy announced the Port of Leghorn in its northwestern Genova Bay as a free port in 1547. The first special economic zone[2] emerged after Italy officially designated the Port of Leghorn as a free port in response to the needs of the development of international trade following the birth of the capitalist mode of production. The special economic zones came into being and developed along with the generation and development of capitalism and are the product of the commodity economy and international trade development.

The special economic zones grew out of nothing, from few to many, from low levels to high levels in the historical process of the development of special economic zones around the world. Initially, special economic zones were available in small quantities and mainly served foreign trade and entrepôt trade. After the Second World War, their number greatly increased and they focused on developing the export processing industry. Since the 1970s, they have transferred to high levels and have been mainly engaged in developing cutting-edge technologies and technological, knowledge-intensive products. In the 1980s, there was a trend of comprehensive development, and they grew from trade-oriented, export processing-oriented, technology-oriented special economic zones to integrated special economic zones characterized by an equal emphasis on trade, industry, agriculture and the all-round development of primary, secondary and tertiary industries.

(I) Developmental stages of special economic zones around the world

In general, the development of special economic zones around the world can be divided into the following four stages:

1. Initial stage. Capitalism flourished from the middle of the 16th century to the middle of the 19th century. In order to further prosper the national economy and enhance national economic strength, some capitalist countries with international trade advantages started building ports along the coast of the Mediterranean and in other relevant regions as free ports or free trade zones, such as Hamburg and Bremen in Germany, Copenhagen in Denmark, Porto in Portugal, Dunkirk in

[1]Special economic zone refers to the abbreviated form of Special Economic Development Zone. The name of Special Economic Development Zone varies with different establishment objectives and conditions in various countries. It is exclusively named as special economic zone in China.

[2]The Port of Leghorn is the first special economic zone named as free port in the world and is generally considered as the originator of the special economic zones around the world [1].

France, etc. [2]. At that time, the special economic zones concentrated on developing import and export trade, entrepôt trade, and tried to leverage their geographical advantages and policy advantages, including exemption of customs duty, to attract foreign merchants and merchant ships, thus becoming international distribution centers for commodities.

2. Growth stage. Capitalism developed from free competition to imperialism from the middle of the 19th century to the Second World War. With a view to strengthening commodity exports and capital exports, plundering natural resources in colonies and dependent countries to seize more economic benefits and expand their economic sphere, some imperialist countries unilaterally turned the important ports in some colonies, dependent countries and leased territories into special economic zones for developing import and export trade, entrepôt trade in addition to maintaining and adding some new domestic special economic zones; for example, imperialist France and Britain announced Gibraltar, Singapore, Hong Kong, Pulau Pinang, Aden, Djibouti, etc. as free ports or free trade zones.
3. Vigorous developmental stage. The special economic zones experienced a golden age of development from the Second World War to the 1970s. On the one hand, the new independent countries which had just broken away from suzerains, some developing countries and territories established special economic zones focusing on developing the export processing industry or import and export trade to massively introduce foreign capital and advanced technologies in order to consolidate their political independence and pursue economic prosperity. On the other hand, some developed countries fully utilized the natural resources and cheap labor from developing countries or territories and relentlessly exported capital and labor-intensive industries. Highly influential special economic zones include Panama's Colon Free Zone, Brazil's Free Port of Manaus, Canada's export processing industrial villages, New York's No. 1, San Francisco's No. 3 and No. 3A, Chicago's No. 22 foreign trade zones in USA, Ireland's Shannon Export Processing Zone, South Korea's Masan Export Processing Zone, Singapore's Jurong Industrial Estate, The Philippines' Bataan Export Processing Zone, Sri Lanka's Katunayake Investment Promotion Zone, Thailand's Ladkrabang Export Processing Zone, Malaysia's Bayan Lepas Export Processing Zone, Taiwan's Kaohsiung, Nanzih, Taichung export processing zones, etc.
4. High-level developmental stage. With the surge of the third science and technology revolution and the development of economic globalization, the special economic zones have been in the stage of high-level development since the 1970s. Their prominent feature is that the development of cutting-edge technologies, technological and labor-intensive products has become the center of development in the special economic zones. The famous ones include Silicon Valley in California, USA, Silicon Valley in Scotland, The UK, Tsukuba Science City, Japan, Taiwan Hsinchu Science Park, China, etc.

At present, there are more than 1000 special economic zones around the world, among which about 1/3 are located in developed countries, 2/3 in developing countries or territories. The roles of the special economic zones are increasingly enhanced amid regional and global economic integration.

(II) **classification of special economic zones around the world**

Though the establishment objectives and developmental directions are greatly different among different special economic zones, they are basically classified into the following four categories:

1. Trade-oriented. A trade-oriented special economic zone focuses on developing foreign trade and entrepôt trade for obtaining commercial interests. Free ports, free trade zones, free border zones, bonded warehouse zones, foreign trade zones fall within this category.
2. Export processing-oriented. An export processing zone refers to a certain area designated as a special economic zone in a country (territory), where preferential economic policies and inexpensive complete factory buildings, water, electricity, roads, communication and other infrastructures are provided to attract foreign investors to set up factories, develop the export processing industry with competitive power on the international market, from which products are mainly exported.
3. Integrated type. An integrated special economic zone means a large-scale multi-tier, multifunctional special economic zone which is dominated by one industry and is involved in diversified operations. Besides the development of foreign trade and an emphasis on the production of the export industry, it is also engaged in various industries including finance, real estate, tourism, agriculture and animal husbandry, science and technology, culture and education, health and services.
4. Science and technology-oriented. A science and technology-oriented special economic zone is also called a knowledge-intensive zone, a science park, a science city, a high and new technology industrial development zone, etc. It refers to a special economic zone which closely integrates scientific research, production and education, and focuses on developing cutting-edge technology industries and products. Such a kind of special economic zone offers various preferential policies to highly centralize wisdom and capital and specializes in the development of emerging industries involving research, pilot scale tests and the production of new technologies and high technologies.

2 Background of the Times for the Establishment of China's Traditional Special Economic Zones

For ease of research on China's special economic zones, we classify the special economic zones into traditional special zones and new special zones. The former refers to the five special zones established in the 1980s and named special economic zones, including Shenzhen, Zhuhai, Shantou, Xiamen and Hainan, while the latter includes the Pudong New Area, the Binhai New Area, state-level high-tech zones, export processing zones, bonded zones, bonded port zones, the Kashgar Economic Development Zone, the Khorgos Development Zone, the China (Shanghai) Pilot Free Trade Zone, etc. established since the 1990s.

Given the developmental history of the special economic zones around the world, the special economic zones came into being and developed along with the generation and development of Capitalism. Why did China, as a socialist country, establish special economic zones? Why did China not establish special economic zones until the 1980s? Was the establishment of China's special economic zones the sudden impulse of high-level policymakers at that time or the inevitable choice of history? In order to gain a deep understanding of the above questions, we take the international background and domestic background as the longitude and latitude, respectively, to depict the background of the times for establishing China's special economic zones.

(I) The International background: formation of the traditional socialist mode and its dilemma

The contradictions between the traditional economic and political system defended by Socialism and the development of productive forces were increasingly intense in the late 1970s and the early 1980s. At that time, agriculture, light and heavy industries were seriously disproportionate in the national economy; the growth rate of economic development dramatically decreased, the necessities for people's lives were severely undersupplied in the Soviet Union. Many eastern European countries became debt-ridden, where economic development was stagnant, inflation was severe, the people's living standard greatly declined, and national relations were increasingly strained. When the world's socialist system was gradually trapped in severe economic plight, major Western capitalist countries were dedicated to carrying out a high-tech revolution and accelerating the internationalization of capital.

As traditional Socialism got into trouble but Capitalism thrived rather than die away, some socialist builders wandered, but most were finding the way. The first country which challenged the traditional socialist mode was Yugoslavia. The 20th Congress of the Communist Party of the Soviet Union criticized Stalin's personality cult in the mid 1950s. Afterwards, the eastern European countries rose to object the Soviet Union's control and broke the traditional mode. The Polish Incident and Hungarian Incident were the typical cases in that period. The Socialist countries in Eastern Europe triggered a wave of reforms, marked by the Prague Spring, since the 1960s. Faced with the "centrifugal" tendency, the Soviet Union outrageously sent troops to invade and curb the situation; as a result, reforms were suspended in the socialist countries of Eastern Europe.

In the late 1970s and the early 1980s, the traditional socialist mode remained in deep waters; the economic, political and national contradictions increasingly worsened in the Soviet Union, and the authority of the Communist Party of the Soviet Union was weakening, while the voice of reform for breaking the traditional socialist system became an irresistible trend. This reform was not merely the theoretical and policy adjustment and the improvement made by the Communist Party;

instead, it involved complicated international and domestic class struggles and national struggles. The first opposition party, the Polish Solidarity Union, appeared in a socialist country governed by the Communist Party. With this reform, the Soviet Union and the socialist countries in Eastern Europe saw the result: politically, Western-style multi-party parliamentary democracy was practiced; economically, the market economy with privatization as a goal was carried out; the social system was thoroughly transformed from Socialism to Capitalism. Bewilderingly, this reform started with improving the socialist system but ended with abandoning it.

(II) Domestic background: formation of the planned economic system and its disadvantages

With the basic completion of three major socialist transformations and the expansion of the scale of economic development, the disadvantage that rigid and excessive control was exercised in the economic system gradually surfaced. The Central Committee of the Communist Party of China was aware of these problems and put forward some improvement measures before and after the 8th National Congress of the Communist Party of China in 1956; but there was a lack of experience in the construction of Socialism, especially several unrealistic fixed ideas about Socialism formed over a long period time due to the "left" thought within the Party after 1957. Even the correct measures for invigorating enterprises and developing the socialist commodity economy were criticized as Capitalism. Consequently, the excessive centralization in the economic system could not be resolved over a prolonged period of time and became more and more prominent. Although powers were delegated many times during this period, adjustments were limited to the administrative authority of the Central Government and local governments and did not touch upon critical issues concerning the autonomy of enterprises, planning and market, thus actions could not go beyond the rigid rules of the original planned economic system.

Major drawbacks to the original planned economic system were reflected as follows: the government's responsibilities were not separated from those of the enterprises; the Party played the roles of the government; the government made decisions which should have been made by the enterprises; there were barriers between the higher and the lower levels or between different departments and regions; regional protectionism was prevalent; the State exercised excessive control over the enterprises; the roles of commodity production, value law and market were ignored, even denied; equalitarianism was very severe in distribution. Certainly, enterprises lacked the due autonomy and shared the "big pot" of the State, while employees relied on the "big pot" of enterprises, thus severely depressing the enthusiasm of enterprises and employees for production, and largely devitalizing the socialist economy which should be full of vigor.

(III) Undertaking our own path to build socialism with Chinese characteristics

In December, 1978, the Communist Party of China convened the epoch-marking Third Plenary Session of the 11th Central Committee of the Communist Party of China, which established the opening up as a long-term basic national policy. At the National Theory-Discussing Meeting in March, 1979, Deng Xiaoping pointed out:

"The democratic revolution in the past was conducted according to China's conditions by undertaking the path of encircling the cities from the countryside carved out by Comrade Mao Zedong, now we should also proceed from China's conditions to take a Chinese style road to modernization" [3]. The Communist Party of China convened the 12th National Congress in September, 1982, which specified the guiding thought for building socialism with Chinese characteristics. In his opening speech, Deng Xiaoping made a programmatic incisive exposition about the great undertaking of China's reform and opening up: "Our construction modernization must proceed from China's actual conditions, we should learn and draw upon the experience of foreign countries, both in revolution and in construction; however, success will never come if we mechanically copy the experience and the mode from foreign countries. We have had many lessons in this regard. We should combine the universal truth of Marxism with China's actual situation to undertake our own path towards building socialism with Chinese characteristics, which is the basic conclusion drawn by us after summarizing long-term historical experience" [4].

Undertaking our own path towards building socialism with Chinese characteristics means that the construction modernization in socialist China, we should neither copy the traditional socialist mode nor follow the path adopted by the Soviet Union and Eastern Europe; we should go along a socialist road with Chinese characteristics and a national character which conforms to China's national conditions.

(IV) Establishing special economic zones: a breakthrough in China's reform and opening up

China is a vast country with a large population, where the level of productive forces was low and the development was extremely unbalanced among regions. In order to minimize the transaction costs for reform and opening up and to avoid great social frictions and percussions after 30 years of isolation, first it was essential to seek a breakthrough.

Guangdong Province put forward the conception of establishing special economic zones in Guangdong Province in January, 1979. China Merchants of the Ministry of Communications first designated a land lot at Shekou Commune in Baoan County, Guangdong Province, separated from Hong Kong by only a strip of water, to set up the Shekou Industrial Zone. During the Working Conference of the Central Committee held in Beijing in April, 1979, the persons chiefly in charge of Guangdong Provincial Party Committee, Xi Zhongxun and Yang Shangkun reported the work to the Central Committee and suggested: "As Guangdong is adjacent to Hong Kong and Macau, we can leverage this advantage to do something in opening up." Deng Xiaoping immediately responded: "We can designate an area called a special zone" [5].

After this Working Conference of the Central Committee, according to Deng Xiaoping's suggestion, Gu Mu, Secretary of the Secretariat of the Central Committee of the Communist Party of China, Vice Premier of the State Council, led a working group to inspect Guangdong Province and Fujian Province, conducted a careful survey and feasibility study on the establishment of special economic zones together with leaders of both provinces and experts, while both provinces separately reported study results to the Central Committee. After a careful study, on July 15, 1979, the Central Committee of the Communist Party of China and the State Council approved, in writing, the reports of both provinces and officially consented to designate part of the areas in Guangdong's Shenzhen, Zhuhai, Shantou and Fujian's Xiamen as a pilot establishment of a Special Export Zone. For arrangements, the Central Committee believed that pilot work could be carried out first in Shenzhen and Zhuhai. After experience was accumulated, considerations were given to establish Shantou and Xiamen as Special Export Zones.

Shenzhen was the first to be established as a Special Export Zone among the four special zones. The Shekou Industrial Zone was the first to start construction in Shenzhen. Its construction began in July, 1979; it was called "Test Tube Special Zone". The initial name—Special Export Zone—was mainly designed to differentiate it from the name "Export Processing Zone" in capitalist countries. In March, 1980, the Central Committee of the Communist Party of China convened the working conference of Guangdong Province and Fujian Province in Guangzhou to sum up the progress in implementing special policies in foreign economic activities and preparing the pilot establishment of special export zones in both provinces; they also discussed some specific measures for establishing the special economic zones. Afterwards, Deng Xiaoping proposed to change the name "Special Export Zone" to "Special Economic Zone". The Standing Committee of the National People's Congress adopted and promulgated the Regulations on Special Economic Zones in Guangdong Province ("the Regulations") on August 26, 1980. The Regulations provided that in order to develop foreign economic cooperation and technical exchanges and promote socialist modernization, certain areas in Guangdong's Shenzhen, Zhuhai and Shantou were separately designated as special economic zones. Special zones encourage foreign citizens, overseas Chinese, compatriots from Hong Kong and Macao and their companies, and enterprises to invest in and set up factories or cooperate with us to establish joint-venture factories, set up enterprises and carry out other undertakings, and protect the profits attributable to their assets and other legal income in accordance with laws. Meanwhile, the first special economic zone in China—Shenzhen Special Economic Zone, officially came into being. The construction of the Zhuhai Special Economic Zone officially commenced in October, 1980. Ground was broken for the Xiamen Special Economic Zone in October, 1981. The construction of the Shantou Special Economic Zone also began in November, 1981. Hainan Special Economic Zone was established on April 13, 1988.

3 Transformation of China's Special Economic Zones in the New Period

The background of the "altruistic" establishment of traditional special economic zones determines that special zones serve as "windows", "experimental fields", models and drivers, and the special zones are national special zones. While enjoying the "trial and error" privilege, the special economic zones assume the historical mission of reducing the risks and costs of the national reform and opening up and paving the way for them. When the market-oriented reform of the special zones becomes the goal for national reform—the establishment of socialist market economy system, the historical mission of traditional special economic zones has basically been accomplished. At this time, the special zones are national special zones and also their own special zones. Special zones are designed for "altruistic" experimentation, and more importantly, the special zones present their own "mutually beneficial" growth.

(I) **Functional positioning of traditional special economic zones**

1. Special economic zones are the windows on China's reform and opening up
   At the beginning of the establishment of China's special economic zones, Deng Xiaoping stressed that special economic zones should be closely connected with the expansion of national reforms and the opening up. In his first inspection of the special economic zones in 1984, Deng Xiaoping stated: "The special zones are windows—windows for technology, management and knowledge as well as external policies" [6]. With the near absence of capital support from the Central Government, the special economic zones earnestly introduced foreign capital, attracted advanced technologies and management experience from foreign enterprises, thus saving the national fiscal funds, achieving rapid development and stimulating the economic development of the surrounding areas.
2. The special economic zones are the experimental fields for the reform of China's economic system
   In order to build socialism with Chinese characteristics, it is unfeasible to take the traditional socialist road and copy the Western mode; instead, it is essential to push forward institutional reform so as to find a socialist modernization road suitable to China's national conditions. Reform entails costs. Failure to succeed in reform may cause economic losses, even social turbulence. Therefore, it is necessary to find a suitable area to carry out reform experiments in before large-scale reform can effectively avoid potential risks. The special economic zones are the frontiers of reform and the opening up and are the forerunners of China's economic development, thus it is relatively easy for them to draw upon foreign advanced managerial experience; furthermore, they are less subject to the restraints of the old system and the Central Government gives them special policies, thus they are most appropriate for acting as experimental fields for reform and opening up. If the reform is successful, the reform experience can be applied nationwide; if the reform fails, its impact is only limited to a small scope and it will not produce great negative effects nationwide.
3. The special economic zones serve as the bridges for promoting the peaceful reunification with the motherland
   The establishment of special economic zones including Shenzhen, Zhuhai, Shantou, Xiamen and Hainan contains the political vision for promoting peaceful reunification with the motherland. Traditional special economic zones

have played an important role in securing the return of the sovereignty of Hong Kong and Macau, subsequently maintaining their prosperity and stability after their return, promoting peaceful reunification with the motherland, safeguarding the national unity and stabilizing the situation of the South China Sea.

4. The special economic zones serve as models and drivers
   Instead of adopting the mode of small area and single functional structure in most of special economic zones around the world, China's special economic zones have successfully undertaken the path towards developing large-scale, outward-looking integrated special economic zones. The main task at the inception of special zones was to develop their own economy. After the special zones developed and grew economically, they played a radiation effect on and stimulated the economy in the areas surrounding them and the hinterland. Shenzhen Special Economic Zone has developed from a small border town into the model of China's special economic zones in more than 30 years. Shenzhen Special Economic Zone has gradually shifted some industries to its surrounding areas, including Dongguan and Huizhou, since the early 1990s, thus driving the development of the local economy. Shenzhen has also helped part of the hinterland develop its economy through investment and assistance.

(II) The functional transformation of the special economic zones in the new period

As China has increasingly integrated into the economic globalization and the degree of its economic openness has been on the increase, an all-round opening-up pattern has taken shape; the mission of traditional special zones as the windows for the opening up has been basically accomplished. As reform and opening up are intensifying, the reforms of the political and economic systems are also carried out nationwide, and the traditional special zones are no longer the first choice as the experimental fields for institutional reform, while some reforms such as the coordinated development of urban and rural areas cannot be launched in the traditional special zones. The role of traditional special zones as the experimental fields is gradually weakening, while the enthusiasm of other areas for seeking experimentation is rising. Given the current development of traditional special zones and the developmental situation of the national economy, the historical mission of traditional special economic zones has basically been completed and the special zones are at a new crossroads of development.

The French economist François Perroux believes that a balanced development is realistically impossible in a country or territory; in general, economic growth is gradually transmitted to other areas through one or several economic growth centers, thus the government should adopt relevant policies to consciously allocate growth poles for stimulating the development of relevant industries or areas.

As China is a vast country, the natural conditions, the geographical locations, history, culture and other factors are different among areas across China. This determines that China's regional development cannot be fostered by a single national balanced developmental strategy. Limited resources should be used in a specific area to develop it in advance of other areas in China, and then the area which becomes prosperous first promotes the development of the backward areas. Such a strategy lays stress on giving priority to efficiency while considering equity in economic development. This is the inevitable choice of an overall strategy for regional economic development in China.

4 Coordinated Development of the Special Economic Zones and the Non-special Zones in the Transformation Period

With 35 years of explorations and practice, as the forerunners of China's reform and opening up, the special economic zones have grown into a developmental model—the special economic zone model. The background of the "altruistic" establishment of traditional special economic zones determines that the special zones basically function as the "windows" and "experimental fields" for reform and opening up, and they are national special zones rather than their own special zones. When the socialist market economy system, successfully experimented in the special zones, becomes the goal for national reform and opening up, the historical mission of traditional special zones will have basically been accomplished. The convening of the Third Plenary Session of the 18th Central Committee of the Communist Party of China marked China's entry into a new developmental period for a comprehensively intensified reform and opening up. The establishment of the China (Shanghai) Pilot Free Trade Zone means that the development of China's special economic zones has entered the transformation period, during which the special economic zones face the following two major difficulties: First, how special economic zones leverage appropriate advantages to further promote their development; second, how to coordinate the development of special economic zones and non-special zones. Obviously, the latter attracts attention from all sectors of society under the current situation since the coordinated development of special economic zones and non-special zones has a bearing not only on the balanced development of China's regional economy, but also on the income distribution, social justice and even on social stability.

(I) Functional transformation of the special economic zones in the transformation period

1. The evolution of the form of special economic zones
   China's special economic zones can be divided into traditional special economic zones and emerging special economic zones according to the historical developmental process and historical missions. Traditional special economic zones refer to the five special zones established in the 1980s and named special economic zones, which were Shenzhen, Zhuhai, Shantou, Xiamen and Hainan, and which represent a milestone due to their roles as the windows and

experimental fields for China's reform and opening up. Emerging special economic zones mean the economic areas where the State has implemented special policies for developing the regional economy and coordinating the regional development since the 1990s, such as the Pudong New Area of Shanghai, the Binhai New Area of Tianjin, the Kashgar Economic Development Zone, etc. [7]. Although these different kinds of "special zones" are not named special economic zones, they aim at addressing some major difficulties in the reform of the economic system; essentially, they remain special economic zones regardless of their different functions.

2. Functional transformation of the special economic zones
   The traditional special economic zones basically function as the windows for reform and opening up, the experimental fields for the reform of the economic system, the bridges for promoting national peaceful reunification, models and drivers. With the intensification of reform and the opening up, the mission of the special economic zones as the windows for the opening up has been accomplished. Meanwhile, the reforms of the political and economic systems are carried out in full swing nationwide. Traditional special economic zones are no longer the first choice as the experimental fields for institutional reforms, and their role as experimental fields is gradually declining, while there is an increasing enthusiasm from other areas for serving as experimental fields.

The developmental experience of the traditional special economic zones, including Shenzhen, shows that as a kind of special resources, special policies can become the important driving forces for the economic development of a region and turn them into the economic growth pole for that region, so as to stimulate the economic development of other areas within the region, even in other regions; moreover, after preferential policies are universally applied, they still maintain rapid economic growth and continue to play the leading role. The developmental process of the traditional special economic zones implies a developmental model: a city, a city group, or a city circle within a certain region can be chosen as a pole, and the State provides special policies (including certain preferential policies) to that city, city group, or city circle and makes it into a special economic zone for developing ahead of other regions, and so producing a radiation effect to stimulate the economic development of other regions, in order to narrow the gap in the level of economic development within a region and among regions. In the transformation period, the special economic zones are no longer pure experimental fields for reform and opening up; though experiment remains an important function of theirs, the special economic zones are mainly designed to promote regional development, and the main function of the new special zones has been substantively changed. The new special zones are established and relevant special policies are given so that the region can further attract factor agglomeration, boost their economic development, generate a polarization effect and then exert a diffusion effect, which has become a new regional developmental model [8].

(II) Problems in the developmental practice of special economic zones and non-special zones

China's implementation of the regional economic developmental strategy is generally divided into the following three stages: [9].

The first stage: the 1950s to the 1970s. A balanced regional economic developmental strategy was implemented under the rigid planned economic system. Facts prove that such a strategy can achieve a certain success in the initial period after new China was founded, but it runs counter to the economic efficiency principle for comparative advantages, and the planned economy can hardly bear information asymmetry, resulting in low efficiency and failure of such a strategy.

The second stage: the 1980s. A non-balanced developmental strategy with the special economic zones as growth poles was adopted against the general background of reform and the opening up. Under the principle of giving priority to efficiency, Deng Xiaoping advocated that part of the people, part of the regions were allowed to prosper first. In that period, China established five traditional special economic zones, Shenzhen, Zhuhai, Shantou, Xiamen and Hainan, and these special economic zones became de facto growth poles. They rapidly developed through the polarization effect and exerted a positive impact on their surrounding areas, even nationwide through the diffusion effect. With the successful implementation of such a strategy, China maintained a high-speed growth for more than 20 consecutive years, which is hailed as a miracle in the history of economic development in the world.

The third stage: the 1990s until now. Guided by the theory of gradient transfer, a non-balanced coordinated developmental strategy has been put into practice—increasing emphasis has been placed on balanced and coordinated regional development while paying attention to regional non-balanced development. As from the 8th Five-Year Plan, especially in the later period of the 9th Five-Year Plan and the 10th Five-Year Plan period, China carried out a series of strategies for non-balanced coordinated development; the establishment of the Pudong New Area, the development of the western regions, the revitalization of the northeastern old industrial base, the rise of Central China, the establishment of different kinds of special economic zones all involve balanced development based on non-balanced development.

However, as great achievements have been made by adopting a non-balanced developmental strategy in the special economic zones, unavoidable problems have arisen, especially circulative accumulation has led to particularly salient problems in the coordinated development of the special economic zones and non-special zones.

1. The polarization effect from the special economic zones has turned out to be obviously negative

   As the regional economic growth poles, special economic zones can, by virtue of the scale economy driven by them, produce a strong polarization effect on labor, capital, technology and other factors in the surrounding areas. When such a polarization effect is stronger than its diffusion effect, the developmental opportunities in the surrounding areas will be deprived and such deprivation tends to intensify, thus the economic development disparities between special zones and non-special zones will become increasingly apparent, causing the structure of a "geographically dual economy".

In the long term, the polarization effect will not always be stronger than the diffusion effect, the growth will not infinitely accumulate, and the geographical diffusion effect (trickle-down effect) will be sufficient to narrow the gap among regions. However, the problem is how long the polarization effect will be stronger than the diffusion effect. The diffusion effect of a growth pole is undeniable, but the polarization stage is undoubtedly long; in such a long time, political instability factors caused by regional developmental imbalance may increase.

2. The possibility that the "enclave type" special zones might emerge is increasing
   Compared with the traditional special zones, the new special zones are generally designed for modern industry or service industry. They have advanced the technical equipment and management methods, but require high innovation capabilities. These industries do not offer many employment opportunities for the surrounding areas, with an obvious minor diffusion effect. As a result, the "enclave type" special zones, unrelated to the development of the surrounding areas, appear, and it can be predicted that it is less likely that such "enclave type" special zones can produce a diffusion effect in the long run. They fail to act as growth poles for regional economic development, and they can even exacerbate the imbalance of regional economic development.
3. Competition involving local interests aggravates the polarization effect of the special zones
   Driven by dual interests—fiscal and tax decentralization, an economic evaluation system—fierce competition has formed among local governments since the reform and the opening up. Such competition has an increasingly negative impact while pushing forward sustained rapid economic growth in China.
   Such competition among local governments also covers the competition between the governments of special economic zones and that of non-special zones. In the new period, special economic zones are still given the power for first implementation and experimentation and still shoulder heavy responsibility for serving as the vanguard in intensifying the national reform and opening up; however, the special economic zones face the challenges that policy-related comparative advantages decrease and their characteristics fade away. Reinforcing their own development will be the first priority for the special zones. In other words, the primary goal for the special economic zones, as independent interest bodies amidst intense regional competition, will lie in further developing themselves, followed by considering the coordinated development with non-special zones. The governments of special zones should proceed from their own interests and take the following actions: First, using their special statuses, continue seeking from the Central Government the

regional policies beneficial for them; second, leveraging their existing strong positions in the regional economy to develop local policies favorable to them. Both actions will strengthen the polarization effect on non-special zones to further deprive developmental opportunities from non-special zones.

4. A segmented regional market hinders the diffusion effect of the special zones
   The coordinated development of the special economic zones and the non-special zones needs to be achieved by the diffusion effect from the special economic zones on the non-special zones. At present, two basic patterns in China's market system obviously obstruct such a diffusion effect.
   On the one hand, regional protectionism driven by local interests is so rampant that the regional market is segmented and the normal flows on the commodity market and factor market are severely impeded. On the other hand, subject to administrative monopolies and control by vested interest groups, the market mechanism is seriously distorted, thus the diffusion effect from the special zones on the non-special zones is delayed or will not occur at all. Both actual patterns exacerbate the imbalance between the special economic zones and the non-special zones.

(III) Thinking of policies concerning the coordinated development of special economic zones and non-special zones

According to the economist Karl Gunnar Myrdal et al., a strong intervention from the government is necessary for advancing the coordinated development of regional economy. Given the problems from the practice in China's special economic zones and non-special zones, the key to promoting the coordinated development of both lies in ensuring the smooth progress of the spread of the special economic zones.

1. Develop a unified fair market system
   The market system centers on price and is governed by the principle of efficiency. Market competition more often tends to incur non-uniformity, difference and exacerbation of such a tendency. Even so, the market is the most effective way for realizing the diffusion effect from the special economic zones on the non-special zones. The market is the foundation for resource allocation and coordinated regional development. Market barriers, segmented markets and regional blockades are the important causes for hindering the diffusion effect. As the reform of economic system advanced regionally, the degrees of economic marketization were different among regions in China, which is also the important cause for intensifying regional economic differences in the transition period.
   Therefore, a consistent environment for the market economic system among regions is the basic prerequisite for coordinated development of the regional economy. Only after a regional blockade is removed, various rules concerning market segmentation, which are detrimental to fair competition, are abolished, and administrative barriers are broken to establish a domestic uniform market for facilitating the flow of various factors, can the institutional foundation

become available for the diffusion effect from the special economic zones on the non-special zones and the coordinated development of both can be smoothly achieved.

2. Strengthen the role conversion and functional innovation of the government
   Role conversion and functional innovation of the government is a systematic issue. When the Central Government delegates powers, due to the lack of an effective restraint mechanism and control means for regulating the acts of local governments, the economic power of local governments is magnified, and even this gives rise to the fact that the local economy is led by local governments, thus begetting many drawbacks, including administrative barriers, local protectionism, market restrictions, vicious competition, ineffective investments, even violent corruption, eventually causing the market to be driven out of the rules of the game. Practice proves that the government should be and is restricted to performing the following four basic functions: protecting private property rights, supplying public products, providing basic social security and providing a just and fair social environment. If the special economic zones enjoy certain advantages due to their location and policies, the government-led economy may cause excessive and improper polarization of production factors from the surrounding areas towards the special economic zones, thus the developmental opportunities in the surrounding areas will be artificially deprived.
   The role of the government and functional innovation is the foundation for the market mechanism to play its role, and also makes up the basic guarantee for establishing a unified, fair market system—producing a diffusion effect. Two forces including the government and the market rise and decline in turn. Both theory and practice prove that the leading role of the market is unshakable. The role of the government and functional innovation is one of the reform priorities for China in the future.
3. Take comparative advantage as the primary principle for establishing the special economic zones
   The establishment of special economic zones artificially reinforces certain comparative advantages. The forms of special economic zones are determined according to comparative advantages. Diverse regional comparative advantages certainly diversify the forms of the special economic zones. Only special economic zones established on the principle of comparative advantages can generate the diffusion effect to the greatest extent so that they can stimulate the coordinated development of the surrounding areas and avoid "enclave type" special zones while bringing about their own rapid development.
   The principle of comparative advantage considered in establishing special economic zones mainly involves the industrial level. The industries to be driven by special economic zones should be chosen according to resource endowment, factor conditions and the level of economic development in the surrounding areas; otherwise, there is an extremely high possibility that "enclave type"

special zones will occur, which is contrary to the goal for establishing special economic zones.

4. Improve the cooperation mechanism between special economic zones and non-special zones
   In order to achieve the coordinated development between special economic zones and non-special zones, it is imperative to develop a cooperation mechanism. Such cooperation mechanism may take into account the following three levels: first, the governments of the special economic zones and those of the non-special zones engage in policy cooperation; the regional economic cooperation mechanism is elevated to a legal level; regional economic policies and local industrial policies with legal effect are made; full play is given to the role of the market mechanism to promote the free flow of production factors among regions. This is the starting point for establishing a cooperation mechanism between the special economic zones and the non-special zones.
   Second, the principle of comparative advantages is followed to conduct a rational industrial division between the special economic zones and the non-special zones; blind competition and repeated construction resulting from local interests is not allowed, otherwise, resources are ineffectively utilized. This is the principle for establishing a cooperation mechanism between the special economic zones and the non-special zones.
   Third, after the special economic zones develop for a certain period of time, there are needs for upgrading the industrial structure, and some industries and enterprises which lose comparative advantages in the special economic zones entail gradient transfer towards the non-special zones. Such gradient transfer is exactly the contents and goal for establishing a cooperation mechanism between the special economic zones and the non-special zones.

5 Developmental Model of the Special Economic Zones

(I) Connotation of the mode

In the Modern Chinese Dictionary, "mode" is explained as the standard form of a thing or the standard style which can be followed by people. From the perspective of philosophy, "mode" can also be defined as the unfolding of the inner mechanism of a thing, and it can systematically reflect the essential attributes of a thing in various ways. Overall, "mode" mainly presents three connotations and characteristics: first, internality—mode shows the internal essence of a thing; second, externality—mode is manifested in many forms; third, usable for reference—mode can be learnt and used for reference.

With the advance of developmental economics and the modern economic growth theory, when studying economic development and growth issues concerning certain countries and territories, some experts and scholars always summarize the developmental experience and paths from these countries and territories as one mode.

China has witnessed multiple developmental models since the reform and the opening up, such as an all-round contract in rural areas, a system of economic responsibility in urban areas, the Sunan Mode, the Wenzhou Mode, the Shunde Mode. However, these modes have only a periodical and a local impact nationwide, and the mode which is universally applicable nationwide is unavailable. The special economic zones have exerted a long-term, overall impact on the national economic system and economic development. The special economic zones have become a new mode for China's development.

(II) The special economic zone model

As indicated by the developmental experience from traditional special zones including Shenzhen, as a kind of special resources, special policies can become the important driving forces for the economic development of a region and turn them into the economic growth pole for that region, so as to drive the economic development of other areas within the region, even other regions; moreover, after preferential policies are universally applied, they still maintain a rapid economic growth and continue playing the leading role. The developmental process of traditional special economic zones implies a development model: a city, a city group, or a city circle within a certain region can be chosen as a pole, and the State provides special policies (including certain preferential policies) to that city or city group, or city circle and makes it into a special economic zone to develop ahead of other regions, and then produces a radiation effect to stimulate the economic development of other regions, so as to narrow the gap in the level of economic development within a region and among regions. In this sense, the special economic zones no longer mainly function as the windows for the opening up, the experimental fields for institutional reform; instead, they serve as a regional developmental model to become the pole for the economic growth of the region.

Functionally, the comprehensive reform pilot zones developed by China in the 21st century are different from the traditional special economic zones. These new special zones were established amid the emergence of national level regional developmental strategies for the development of the western regions, the revitalization of the northeastern old industrial base, the rise of Central China. The Pudong New Area of Shanghai and the Binhai New Area of Tianjin are the representatives of coastal new special zones. They take up the heavy responsibility of further developing the outward-looking economy, pushing the economy to transform from an outward-looking one to an open one so as to further make their own economic expansion and thus become the engine for developing China's economy. The Shenbei New Area strives to find a path suitable for developing the northeastern economy and push forward the revitalization of the northeastern old industrial base. The Wuhan City Circle and the Changsha-Zhuzhou-Xiangtan City Circle endeavor to become the vanguard for the rise of Central China. As a region with a better economic foundation in West China, the Chengdu-Chongqing Region mainly aims at balancing urban and rural development, eliminating the urban-rural dual structure, expanding its own economy to promote the post-earthquake economic recovery in the Sichuan region and stimulate the economic development of other areas in West China. In this sense, the special economic zones in the 21st century are no longer pure experimental fields for reform and opening up, although experiment is their main function; the special economic zones are mainly designed to boost the regional economic development, while the main functions of the special zones have been substantively changed. A new regional developmental model arises: new special zones are established and are given relevant special policies to aggregate factors and impel the economic development of the new special zones, produce the polarization effect and then the diffusion effect.

(III) The action mechanism of the special economic zones

Special economic zones are set up to promote the economic growth of a regional central city or a region and first turn it into a pole for regional economic growth; after the special economic zones become economically powerful, they stimulate the economic development of the surrounding areas. The impact from special economic zones on regional economic development is realized through the polarization effect and the diffusion effect.

1. The polarization effect of the special economic zones
   The polarization effect illustrates the process in which the production factors, including capital, talents and technologies, gather in the central city. The special economic zones, as special areas, are slightly different from the ordinary areas in terms of the cause for producing the polarization effect. The polarization effect in the ordinary areas is mainly generated by the market mechanism, while that in the special economic zones results from special institutional arrangements in addition to the market mechanism.
   The establishment of the special economic zones is based on special policies, while special policies are special institutional arrangements. Special policies are dominated by preferential policies, while preferential policies are those policies which can directly deliver economic benefits to investors, such as preferential policies relating to taxes, land and prices. Compared with the surrounding areas, the special economic zones are the policy-oriented low-lying land where entrepreneurs make investments in order to reduce the production costs and where the production factors gather. At the initial stage after its establishment, the Shenzhen Special Economic Zone relied on special policies to attract foreign enterprises, including Hong Kong and Taiwan-funded enterprises.
2. The diffusion effect of the special economic zones
   The diffusion effect means that the areas surrounding the economic center get access to production factors, including capital, talents and technologies, along with the economic expansion of the regional economic center so as to promote the development of the local economy. Thanks to government regulations and the market mechanism, the special economic zones can bring together factors in a short time to expand their own economy and then produce a diffusion effect to motivate the economic development of the surrounding areas. The diffusion effect of the special economic zones works mainly through the

industrial gradient transfer mechanism, the institutional transplantation and imitation mechanism, the knowledge technology spillover mechanism.

(1) The industrial gradient transfer mechanism

As the economy of the special economic zones develops, the local market gradually becomes saturated, and the prices of production factors, including land and labor, are on the rise, thus the costs for enterprises' production operations within the zones increase. Many industries with high pollution and low added value are introduced to the special zones for developing their own economy at the early stage of development. When the economy of the special economic zones develops to a certain level, it is necessary to upgrade the industrial structure, thus these low-end industries start moving to the surrounding areas for survival. As part of industries shift, the areas to which these industries shift see further improvement of the industrial structure, and the industrial linkage effect helps develop related industries, thus promoting the economic development of these areas.

(2) The institutional transplantation and imitation mechanism

This mechanism means that the areas with backward institutional arrangements learn from the areas with advanced institutional arrangements; in other words, advanced institutional arrangements are transplanted, imitated and localized to propel the local economic development. Institutional transplantation and imitation is able to reduce the institutional change costs in the areas with backward institutional arrangements—lowering the institutional searching costs, shortening the time for institutional changes, drawing experience and lessons from the institutionally advantageous areas during the institutional changes.

Institutional changes involve potential risks. A set of rational systems can boost the economic development, while irrational ones will hinder the economic development. Institutional changes are a risky "trial and error" process. A better way to mitigate institutional change risks is that institutional changes should be restricted to a small area and new institutional arrangements should be applied in other areas after such institutional arrangements are proved to be fit for the economic development. Special policies and special management systems constitute the foundation for the existence of the special economic zones. The special economic zones enjoy the power to experiment first, even the "trial-and-error power", thus a loose political environment is available for making institutional changes in the special economic zones. As the special economic zones undertake the task of reform and experimentation, this certainly requires institutional changes, therefore, the special economic zones are located at the high end of institutional arrangements compared with the surrounding areas.

After a set of well-proven systems are developed in the special economic zones, these systems are non-exclusive, thus these systems can be transplanted and imitated by other areas at low costs, and then the actual situation of local economic development is considered to make the institutional arrangements beneficial for local economic development, so as to effectively avoid potential risks in institutional changes and save the costs of those changes.

(3) The technological spillover mechanism
The special economic zones have a technology spillover effect on the surrounding areas mainly by the following means: first, the free movement of people. Some large enterprises within the special zones attach importance to research, development and employee training; once the scientific research and managerial talents of these enterprises flow to the surrounding areas, some enterprises in these areas will benefit from their technologies and managerial aptitude. Second, the demonstration effect of the enterprise development. When part of enterprises within the special zones gain high profits due to advanced technologies and managerial experience, imitation of these enterprises within the special zones by other enterprises in the industry will improve the economic benefits for the enterprises in surrounding areas. Third, the upstream and downstream linkage effect among industries. Some enterprises within the special zones may keep close contacts with the enterprises outside the special zones in the capacity of supplier, customer, partner etc.; they often provide suppliers with training and technical assistance in order to help suppliers enhance the quality of the product. Part of the enterprises in the special zones get into a technical cooperation relationship with enterprises and research institutions of the surrounding areas, also can produce a technological spillover effect.

6 Special Economic Zones and the China Model

In recent years, with the rapid rise of China's economy, "Chinese Times" has gradually replaced the "American Times" to become the mainstream; China has a growing global influence and the China Model has become the hot topic in the international academic circles.

(I) Discussions about the China Model

Opinions about the connotation of the "China Model" are always diverse in the academic circles. Some scholars equate "China Model" with "Beijing Consensus"; some scholars believe that there is difference between them; some scholars discuss neither one nor rethink "China Model" from the perspective of the difference between experience and mode.

Joshua Cooper Ramo published an article entitled "The Beijing Consensus", which kicked off great worldwide attention to the China Model. He believed that the China Model was the Beijing Consensus and summarized the China Model in the following three theorems: innovation, efforts, self-development.

Fan Qiuying [10] held that the China Model was equal to the Beijing Consensus. She thought that the China Model was a developmental model with Chinese characteristics, socialism-oriented, which took harmonious development as its goal, was driven by reform innovation, put the people first and stressed pragmatism.

Yin Qian [11] believed that the China Model was logically higher than the Washington Consensus and the Beijing Consensus. The China Model was a practical experience and a developmental philosophy, with reference to the developmental models of other countries or territories, while the Beijing Consensus was only a developmental philosophy, was relative to the Washington Consensus, and it was a concept equivalent to the Post-Washington Consensus, to the European Value Outlook[3] etc., all of which fell within the scope of developmental philosophy. Therefore, comparatively, the Beijing Consensus represented too narrow a perspective.

Shen Yunsuo [12] defined the China Model from the perspective of a developmental road and experience which referred, in particular, to a social developmental road or developmental experience since China's reform and opening up, and treated China's social developmental road from a globalization or global perspective, which was also called the Chinese road, the Chinese experience.

Li Keqin [13] considered that as a concept, the China Model cannot fully embody the complete connotation of China's reform and opening up. The Chinese Experience was more able to fully show the historical landscape of China's developmental changes since it was open, inclusive, not stereotyped, constantly changed and developed. It respected the experiential selection of other countries, which was not opposite to Western experience, but also did not emphasize its own universal applicability. Li Keqin believed that the Chinese Experience was obviously more rational, mature, objective and just than the China Model.

We believe that the China Model has been a summarization of the developmental experience in various fields, including economy, politics, culture and society, since China's reform and opening up, and it is particularly based on economic reform, while economic reform has been mainly driven and practiced by the special economic zones; thereby, the special economic zone model formed by the developmental paths for traditional special economic zones and new special zones is the foundation and core of the China Model.

(II) The action mechanism of the special economic zones is the motive power for forming the China Model

The imbalance of the economic and social development among regions is a common severe problem for countries around the world, especially large countries. China is a vast country where the population is not commensurate with the level of productive forces, making this problem more prominent. The China Model is highly regarded by most of the developing countries, even a few developed countries, because China has fully considered this problem by specifying the goal:

[3]The European Value Outlook is based on the European traditional philosophy of the value of social democracy and advocates human rights, environmental protection, social security and equitable distribution while emphasizing economic growth.

some of the people and some of the regions are allowed to first prosper and then help the backward regions so as to gradually achieve prosperity for all. This tallies with the law of social and economic development and has a universal value. In order to achieve prosperity for all, the special economic zones are established to promote the economic growth of a main regional city or an entire region and make it become a pole for regional economic growth. After the special economic zones grow economically, they stimulate the development of the surrounding areas, even the national development.

The special economic zones produce a polarization effect to draw in the production factors, including capital, talents and technologies; subsequently, the economic expansion of the central regions generates a diffusion effect to externally diffuse the production factors, including capital, talents and technologies, so as to propel the economic development of the surrounding areas. Special economic policies and special economic management systems gradually develop the special economic zones into a new regional economic developmental model and a good example of the China Model. In a certain period, the special zones witness more remarkable achievements than other areas and secure a favorable competitive position, characterized by a rapid economic growth, a significant improvement in per-capita income, a rapid enhancement of comprehensive strength. Their developmental experience is "copied" from coastal cities to those inland so as to form the China Model.

(III) The special economic zones have created the China Model

The most basic connotation of the China Model is the economic developmental model, which is mainly driven by China's developed areas represented by the special economic zones, thus the special economic zones have created China's economic developmental model, as shown in Fig. 1.

The special economic zone model refers to a developmental path which mainly entails the process of development from traditional special zones named special economic zones to new special zones dominated by new zones, comprehensive reform pilot areas and special economic developmental zones. Other economic areas, established or opened during this process, where special economic policies and special economic management systems were implemented (such as the 14 costal open cities, the coastal economic developmental zones, the national new and hi-tech developmental zones, the national bonded areas and the bonded port areas, the export processing zones, the three large economic circles, the economic developmental zones, the national economic and technological developmental zones, the national key developmental and opening pilot zones) also fall within the scope of the special economic zones. China's economic developmental model is a generalization and summarization of the developmental strategies, ways of thinking, successful experience and practices in the economic development of the special economic zones.

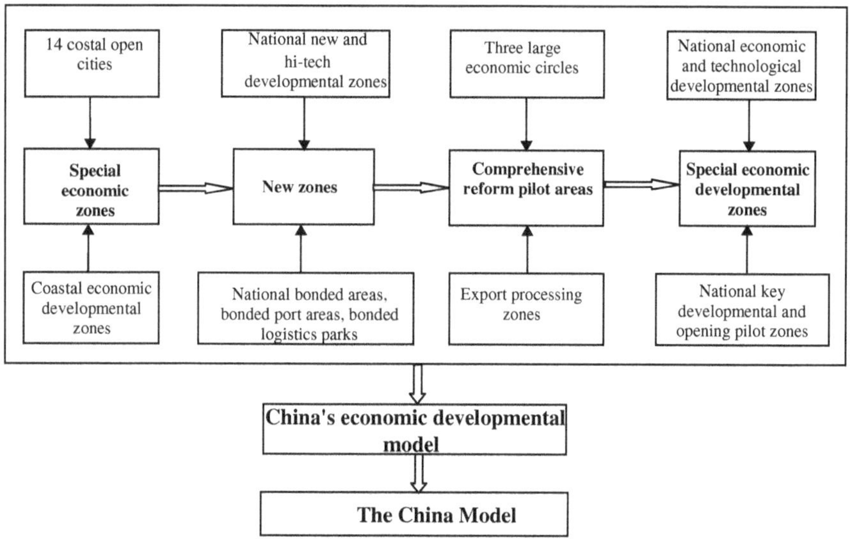

Fig. 1 The path of formation of the China Model

(IV) The special economic zone model is essentially consistent with the China Model

From the establishment of the traditional special economic zones as "windows" and "experimental fields" to the development and opening of new zones to comprehensive reform pilot areas and special economic developmental zones, from Shenzhen, Zhuhai, Shantou, Xiamen, Hainan Special Economic Zone to the Pudong New Area and the Binhai New Area to the gradual opening of coastal cities, border areas, cities along rivers and inland cities, China's economic development and construction modernization have been carried out by adopting the economic gradient developmental strategy from "points" to "lines" and then "areas". The key is the work on "points", and the special economic zones represent the best form of "points". The special zones are the frontier of reform and the opening up and are the "windows" and "experimental fields" for reform and the opening up. The special zones are given the "trial-and-error power" so that experiments are carried out, experience and lessons are summarized to gradually push forward extensive work. As the experimental zones for reform and opening up, the special zones are open to experimentation regarding the socialist road with Chinese characteristics. Based upon the "points"—the special economic zones—he national all-round opening up is promoted. The China Model is gradually formed in this process. In essence, the China Model features reform and opening up.

(V) The special economic zones have boosted the development of the China Model

China has been actively exploring a new market economic system during the reform and the opening up. According to the guidelines of the Central Committee for "blazing a new trail" and "going beyond the existing system", among the special zones, Shenzhen became the first to launch a series of institutional reforms including prices, foreign exchanges, finance and foreign trade, and insisted on introducing something from foreign countries and going global. The special zones made use of special economic policies and special managerial systems to move the opening up forward. Industries, including processing of materials supplied by foreign clients, processing according to buyer's samples, assembling of parts supplied by foreign clients and compensation trade, were introduced; various resource advantages were utilized to develop an outward-looking economy, thus greatly promoting the rapid development of the special economic zones. Foreign capital, technologies, managerial experience and managerial talents were massively introduced to inject new vigor for developing the economy of the special zones. The special zones have acquired rich successful experience from development and serve as the models to be learnt and adopted for the development of other areas. Therefore, various areas have drawn upon the successful experience of the special economic zones to accelerate their own development, thus further pushing the development of the China Model forward.

The China Model has been a summarization of the development experience in various fields, including economy, politics, culture and society, since China's reform and opening up, while the special economic zone model is the foundation and core of the China Model. As "a single spark can start a prairie fire", the special economic zones have rapidly developed through reform and opening up for 35 years, expanding the development from several cities in the eastern coastal areas to the whole of China, including bonded areas, bonded port areas, export processing zones, new and hi-tech developmental zones, economic and technological developmental zones, economic circles, key developmental and opening pilot zones, as a model, to promote the formation and development of the China Model.

References

1. Zhong Jian: *A Study of Developmental Models for the Special Economic Zones around the World*, Beijing, China Economic Publishing House, 2006, p. 3.
2. Luo Qinghe: *Introduction to the Economics of the Special Economic Zones*, Beijing, Central Compilation & Translation Press, 2001, p. 2.
3. *Selected Works of Deng Xiaoping* (Volume 2), p. 163.
4. *Selected Works of Deng Xiaoping* (Volume 3), pp. 2–3.
5. Publicity Department of the Shenzhen Municipal Committee of the Communist Party of China: *Spring of 1992: Deng Xiaoping and Shenzhen*, p. 18, Haitian Publishing House, 1992.
6. Selected Works of Deng Xiaoping (Volume 3), pp. 51–52.

7. Luo Qinghe, Cai Tengfei, Li Pei: Special Economic Zones Remain Special in the New Period (J), *Journal of Shenzhen University* (Humanities & Social Sciences), 2008(11), pp. 21–26.
8. Luo Qinghe: Functional Transformation of the Special Economic Zones in the Transformation Period (N), *Chinese Social Sciences Today* (Economics), August 17, 2010.
9. Yan Pengfei, Shao Qiufen: A Study of the Economic Growth Pole Theory (J), *The Theory and Practice of Finance and Economics*, 2001(3), pp. 2–6.
10. Fan Qiuying et al.: The Connotation of the Beijing Consensus and Its Inspirations, *Journal of Tangshan College*, 2008(1), pp. 33–34.
11. Yin Qian: Explanation of the Concept of the China Model, *Weishi*, 2008(10), pp. 24–27.
12. Shen Yunsuo: *The China Model Theory*, Beijing, People's Publishing House, 2007.
13. Li Keqin: The China Model or the Chinese Experience, *Journal of the Party School of Nanning Municipal Committee of the Communist Party of China*, 2006(2), pp. 44–46.

A Study of the "New Normal" Path for the Shenzhen Special Economic Zone

Zhou Xiaoyun

Abstract This paper follows three basic consensuses about the "new normal" and China's developmental stage corresponding to it, provides a logical analysis of the historical evolution, economic transformation and institutional changes of the Shenzhen Special Economic Zone, and discusses the developmental characteristics of the Shenzhen Special Economic Zone under the "new normal" to put forward suggestions for the choice of a path—pursuing a two-stage, three-level coordinated development, keeping a reasonable range of gap between the secondary and tertiary industries, and fostering the common development of multiple market players.

Keywords New normal · Shenzhen special economic zone · Developmental characteristics · Choice of path

1 Key Contents of the "New Normal" and Research Issues

The term "new normal" was first coined by Mohamed A. El-Erian, CEO at PIMCO. It became one of the special topics at the annual meeting of the 40th Davos World Economic Forum 2010 [1]. The historical background for putting forward the concept of "new normal" is that it is impossible to return to the stable "normal" state before 2008 due to the global financial and economic crisis caused by the US

Zhou Xiaoyun, Vice-dean of the School of Economics and Management, Director of the Center for Small and Medium-sized City Development Research, Xinyu University, Shenzhen University visiting scholar under the "Western Light" Program initiated by the Organizational Department of the Central Committee of the Communist Party of China, Associate Professor, PhD; address: Xinyu University, No. 2666, Yangguang Avenue, Xinyu City. This paper is a phased research result of the soft science and technology program entitled "Evolution of Low-carbon Economic Development and Income Distribution" under Jiangxi Provincial Department of Science and Technology in 2013 (No.: 20131561050001).

Z. Xiaoyun (✉)
School of Economics and Management, Xinyu University, Xinyu, Jiangxi, China

Y. Yuan (ed.), *Studies on China's Special Economic Zones*, Research Series on the Chinese Dream and China's Development Path,
DOI 10.1007/978-981-10-3704-7_7

subprime crisis— it means the painful process of slow, low growth of the world's economy after the global financial crisis.

During his inspection in Henan Province in May, 2014, Chinese President Xi Jinping pointed out that for China's development to remain in the important period of strategic opportunity, we should boost confidence, proceed from the characteristics of the stage of China's current economic development, and adapt to the new normal and maintain a strategic normal mindset [2]. That was the first time that the new generation state leader adopted the "new normal" to explain China's economy at the new developmental stage by making reference to international mainstream viewpoints and conducting a scientific judgment about China's current and future development.

The "New normal" rapidly became an important benchmark in the economic field and triggered investigations and debates in the theoretical circles. In general, there are the following three basic consensuses: first, the economic growth rate will decrease and will be kept at a reasonable range—economic growth is governed by its own developmental law and a sustained high growth is not a normal state of the economy under the resource constraint condition, while a rational economic growth rate is the mainstream of development. Second, it is imperative to transform the economic structure—the industrial structure is dominated by the tertiary industry instead of the secondary industry, and there is a boost from Made in China to Created in China. Third, China's economic development is promoted mainly by intensifying reforms—on the premise of pushing ahead with the reform of the socialist market economic system and giving play to the decisive role of the market; macro control is guided by rational growth at the macro level, while innovation and entrepreneurship are stressed to promote economic growth at the micro level [3, 4].

The explanation of the "new normal" is a scientific judgment based on China's economic developmental stage. However, the current developmental stage of the Shenzhen Special Economic Zone is not fully consistent with the developmental stage upon which such judgment is based. In 2013, Shenzhen's GDP and per-capita GDP hit 1450 billion USD and 22,112 USD, respectively [5]; according to the World Bank's standard [6], Shenzhen reached the highest income level.[1] With over 30 years of development, the Shenzhen Special Economic Zone has rich experience and a developmental environment for intensifying reforms, but it is still at the developmental stage of a comprehensively intensifying reform, and needs to dynamically adapt to national-level "new normal" developmental rules.

---

[1]According to the 9th page of the *World Development Data Manual 2013*, as defined by the World Bank's standard, low-income economies refer to the economies with per-capita gross national income being equal to and lower than 1025 USD in 2011; middle-income economies refer to the economies with per-capita gross national income higher than 1025 USD but lower than 12,496 USD; high-income economies refer to the economies with per-capita gross national income being equal to and higher than 12,496 USD. This paper makes theoretical judgment by replacing per-capita gross national income with per-capita domestic gross market value released by the Shenzhen Bureau of Statistics and making reference to the World Bank's standard.

The differences and dynamic adaptation process at this stage present an issue worthy of in-depth discussion: what "new normal" economic development road should be taken by the Shenzhen Special Economic Zone in consideration of showing the developmental course of the Shenzhen Special Economic Zone and following the developmental trend of the national "new normal". For this purpose, this paper starts from three basic consensuses about the "new normal" to analyze the economic logic of the "new normal" in the Shenzhen Special Economic Zone, and to identify a "new normal" developmental road suitable for it, which is not only the inevitable choice for reform and innovations in the Shenzhen Special Economic Zone, but also a beneficial supplement to and a practical exploration of China's "new normal".

2 Analysis of the Economical Logic for the "New Normal" in the Shenzhen Special Economic Zone

Three basic consensuses about the "new normal", the economic growth range, industrial structural transformation and the intensification of the market economic reform, are taken as benchmark, and the historical evolutional logic, economical transformational logic and institutional change logic are analyzed to explore the developmental experience and basic law in the Shenzhen Special Economic Zone.

(I) Analysis of the historical evolutionary logic in the Shenzhen Special Economic Zone

With over 30 years of development, the Shenzhen Special Economic Zone's GDP grew by nearly 800 times, adjusted for the price factor, from 1980 to 2013. Shenzhen's development of more than 30 years is reviewed below to show the characteristics of the stage of the historical evolution.

According to Fig. 1, Shenzhen's economic growth rate and the total labor productivity growth rate have shown basically the same overall developmental trend in more than 30 years; however, in terms of the amplitude of fluctuation, the year 1997 was an important turning point: generally the annual average economic growth rate was higher than 20% before 1997, and the fluctuation was very violent; the difference between the highest growth rate and the lowest one was about 60%, its development featured a large fluctuation and a high growth; the total labor productivity growth rate also dramatically changed and was negative from 1986 to 1989, and a large fluctuation occurred. After 1997, both indicators maintained a relatively stable, gradually adjusted development, and tended to fall within a reasonable growth range as illustrated by the "new normal"—this implies a very valuable judgment: the Shenzhen Special Economic Zone was within a reasonable growth range after 1997. This perspective indicates that Shenzhen has nearly 14 years of experience in exploring the "new normal".

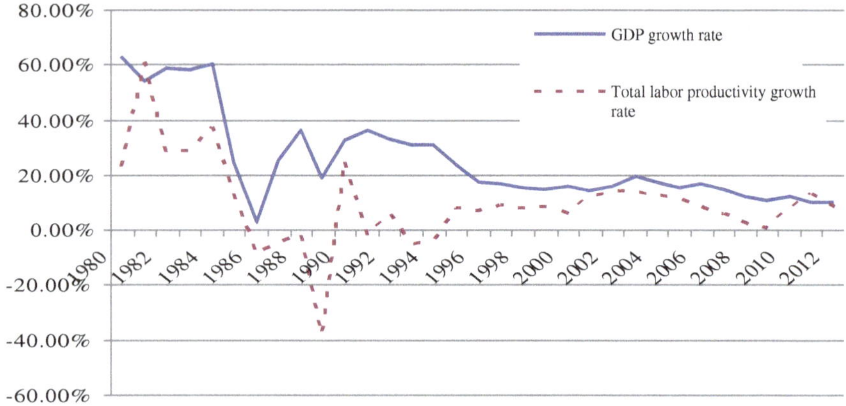

Fig. 1 Shenzhen's economic growth rate and the total labor productivity (Total labor productivity refers to the ratio of gross national product to the total number of employees) growth rate. *Source* Shenzhen Statistical Yearbook 2013

Given this historical evolutionary process, with 1997 as the time node, there may be an occasional cause, but internally it was inevitable—in 1997, Shenzhen's per-capita GDP reached 3000 USD,[2] an important breakthrough, which marked such a situation: Shenzhen's household consumption was shifting from subsistence-focused consumption to affluent consumption, developing from a subsistence type consumption to an enjoyment and developmental type consumption, reaching the level of a middle-income country; the economic growth was transforming from extensive growth to intensive growth. Furthermore, after Hong Kong returned to the motherland in 1997, the market value resulting from the proximity to Hong Kong declined. Especially the Asian financial crisis exerted a great impact on Shenzhen's import and export trade with the Asian countries and territories. These external environmental changes accelerated Shenzhen's transformation towards an endogenous growth pattern.

(II) Analysis of the logic for the economic transformation of the Shenzhen Special Economic Zone

The economic transformational logic is analyzed mainly based on two fields, the industrial structure and the market structure, of the Shenzhen Special Economic Zone to explore and analyze the "new normal" in the transformational practice of the Shenzhen Special Economic Zone.

As indicated by the data in Fig. 2, the overall developmental trend was that the changes in Shenzhen's industrial structure in more than 30 years were dominated by the secondary and tertiary industries, among which the secondary industry grew

[2]Source: *Shenzhen Bureau of Statistics 1998*, Shenzhen's per-capita GDP in 1997 was 25,675 yuan (approximately 3000 USD based on the exchange rate at that time).

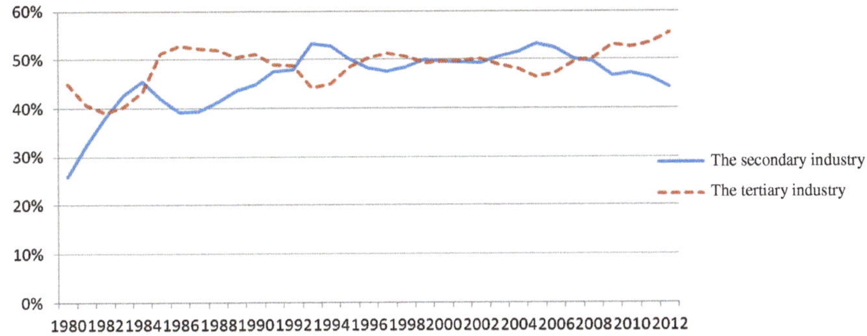

Fig. 2 Proportions of the secondary industry and the tertiary industry in Shenzhen. *Source* Shenzhen Statistical Yearbook 2013

and then declined amid a slight fluctuation, and the tertiary industry generally rose, both mostly accounted for 40–55%. Both took turns eight times in the change of their internal industrial structure: the tertiary industry occupied a relatively long range from 1986 to 2002 and from 2008 to 2013, while the secondary industry took up a relatively long range from 2003 to 2007. Overall, the secondary and tertiary industries alternated many times, and the secondary and tertiary industries maintained a relatively balanced gap in proportion, shaping the characteristic of industrial change in the Shenzhen Special Economic Zone.

This characteristic gives rise to the following two inspirations about the "new normal" of industrial structural transformation: First, the change in the leading position of the secondary and tertiary industries is a dynamic nonlinear process, and alternating development is the important form of the industrial structural optimization and adjustment. Second, the proportions of the secondary and tertiary industries are within a relatively balanced range, and 40% is a lower limit for reference, the main benchmark is that the gap between the proportions of both does not exceed 10%.

According to the data in Fig. 3, domestic enterprises steadily increased and then slowly decreased; foreign-funded enterprises initially grew at a high rate and then slowly rose; generally, private enterprises rapidly increased. Comparison of the three types of enterprises reveals two important nodes: there were more private enterprises than domestic enterprises in 2001, while there were more foreign-funded enterprises than domestic enterprises in 2006. Currently, private enterprises have become the main body of Shenzhen's market structure, in which foreign-funded enterprises and domestic enterprises are the other two market participants.[3] In terms of registered capital, domestic enterprises, foreign-funded enterprises and private enterprises accounted for 10, 3.3 and 86.7%, respectively in 2012; from the

[3]Source: *Shenzhen Statistical Yearbook 2013*, the registered capital of domestic enterprises, foreign-funded enterprises and private enterprises was 190,538.14 million, 64,076.24 million and 1,636,704.90 million USD, respectively in 2012.

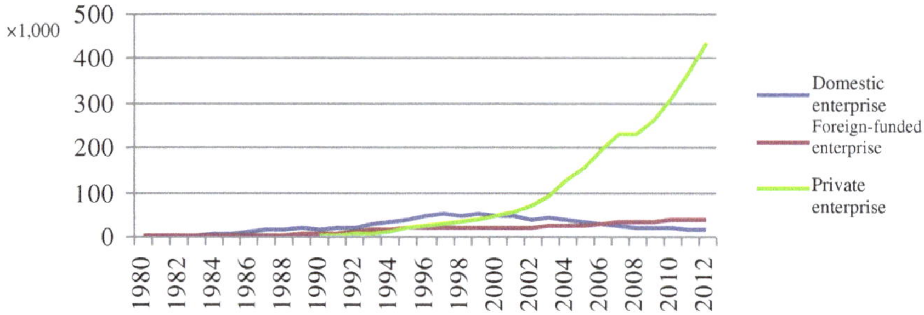

Fig. 3 Number of various enterprises on the Shenzhen market. *Source* Shenzhen Statistical Yearbook 2013. *Note* (This definition comes from the *Shenzhen Statistical Yearbook 2013*, enterprises are classified into domestic enterprise, foreign-funded enterprise and private enterprise by the enterprise registration type) domestic enterprise refers to state-owned enterprises, collective enterprises, joint-equity cooperative enterprises, associated enterprises, limited liability companies, joint-stock limited companies, private enterprises and other enterprises; foreign-funded enterprises refer to the enterprises fully funded and incorporated by foreign investors on the Chinese Mainland according to the Foreign-funded Enterprise Law of the People's Republic of China, relevant laws and regulations; private enterprises refer to private limited liability companies, private join- stock limited companies, private partnership enterprises and private wholly-owned enterprises incorporated by investments from a natural person or controlled by a natural person, including those registered according to the Company Law, Partnership Enterprise Law, Interim Regulations on Private Enterprises

perspective of dynamic development, state-owned enterprises and collective enterprises mainly relied on pushing the development of the market economy, and foreign-funded enterprises served as the important forces to build high competition in the market economy; subsequently, private enterprises heavily depended upon consolidating the developmental foundation for the market economy.

Based on changes in the number of various enterprises and registered capital, a basic profile is identified for the "new normal" of the market structure—domestic enterprises and foreign-funded enterprises are the important parts of the market structure, while private enterprises are the main body of the market structure and develop rapidly. Such a developmental profile means that the "new normal" of the market structure focuses on arousing private innovation and entrepreneurship to enable the rapid development of private enterprises.

(III) Analysis of the logic behind institutional change in the Shenzhen Special Economic Zone

Institutional change is a dynamic process in which a new system or a new system structure replaces or changes the old system. Essentially, this dynamic process entails the replacement of the original system by a more efficient system and a formation of a dependence on a specific path. The more than 30-year development of the Shenzhen Special Economic Zone is also a process in which the socialist market economic system became increasingly mature and perfect, and a process of evolution of "special" and "non-special" institutional arrangements in the special economic zones.

The Shenzhen Special Economic Zone originated from a reform experimentation regarding the original social economic system in China, with the special path of "reform window" adopted to initiate the institutional change in China's socialist market economic system. This reform experimentation with minimum cost broke the traditional planned economic system to take a path of market economy with higher operational efficiency. This dynamic process can be broadly divided into three stages by the logic of the institutional evolution: 1980–1992, 1992–2002, 2002-now.

In 1980, the Shekou Mode heralded an institutional breakthrough; people responded to the philosophy that "time is money, time is efficiency". This opened the gate for institutional change in the Shenzhen Special Economic Zone. The reform philosophy and institutional efficiency swept Shenzhen and a national heated debate on reform and direction of the special zones arouse—whether to establish special zones, whether the reform of special zones should be socialist-oriented or capitalist-oriented, whether to focus on the planned economic system or the market economic system. Such a debate did not stop as a result of the rapid development of the Shenzhen Special Economic Zone; on the contrary, the road to institutional change was followed amid extreme hardship.

Deng Xiaoping's South Inspection Speech in 1992 marked the determination of the developmental direction for institutional change—insisting on the market economic developmental road. This major decision reduced the costs for the institutional change in the Shenzhen Special Economic Zone and quickened the process in which the market economy replaced the planned economy in the Shenzhen Special Economic Zone. It shared similarities with the development during the first stage—the top-down mode was relied on and the government was the most important source and leader of the institutional change; the difference was that the institutional change during the second stage became more orderly and the costs for the institutional change were more controllable, with an emphasis on making the socialist market economic system more systematic and perfect.

An article entitled "Shenzhen, Who Abandoned You" posted online in 2002 [7] stirred a round of debates on the development of the Shenzhen Special Economic Zone in society; it maintained that non-governmental forces had become the important participants in the institutional change in the Shenzhen Special Economic Zone. The year 2002 was the first year for China to observe the WTO rules, a sign that the global rules of the market economy had become the important propellants of the institutional change in the Shenzhen Special Economic Zone. At this stage, the greatest change was that both social and market forces participated in the institutional change and supported the down-top change path. So far, the path towards institutional change in the Shenzhen Special Economic Zone basically involves three reform forces, the government, the society and the market; the internal logic of the efficiency of institutional change leads the Shenzhen Special Economic Zone to the "new normal".

3 The Choice of the Path for the Shenzhen Special Economic Zone under the “New Normal”

As defined by per-capita GDP, Shenzhen has entered a stage of high-income development. In view of the economic growth track, Shenzhen tends to reach a stage of a relatively steady economic growth after a high growth and great fluctuation. From the perspective of the industrial structural change, the secondary and tertiary industries have undergone a cross development three times and have maintained a relatively stable gap in Shenzhen. In regard to market structural change, in Shenzhen, private enterprises have gradually dominated the market, followed by foreign-funded enterprises and domestic enterprises. With respect to the intensification of reforms, the top-down reform mode serves as the starting point and gradually turns into a reform mode with the participation of the government, the society and the market.

Following the developmental evolutionary track of the Shenzhen Special Economic Zone and considering the developmental rules for the national “new normal”, I end this paper with the following three points about the choice of the future path for the Shenzhen Special Economic Zone.

(I) The choice of the path with the two-stage three-level coordinated development of Shenzhen. China’s per-capita gross national income was 4940 USD in 2013, reaching the high and middle-income level [6]. As a relatively independent economy, Shenzhen is at the developmental stage of high-income level. Both stages interweave in Shenzhen’s future development, thus a three-level coordinated development should be sought—coordinated development between the economic growth rate and the quality of economic development, between economic growth and income distribution, between economic growth risks and social transformation.

(II) The choice of a path so that the gap between the secondary and tertiary industries in Shenzhen is kept within a reasonable range. The future choice of a path for the secondary and tertiary industries in Shenzhen should follow the general evolutionary law for the industrial economy in developed countries, and address the gap in proportion to the secondary and tertiary industries, so that early warning and guidance regarding the fluctuation in the gap is given to optimize Shenzhen’s industrial structure. Therefore, Shenzhen should adopt gap fluctuation as the core reference indicator to build a system project consistent with Shenzhen’s industrial policy, thus promoting industrial transformational development in Shenzhen.

(III) The choice of a path regarding Shenzhen’s market economic reform. Efforts should center on innovation and entrepreneurship to further optimize the developmental environment for private enterprises. Reform should focus on mixed ownership and a clear definition of property rights, and the market competition mechanism should be optimized for domestic enterprises. The Negative list management mode should serve as a guide to stimulate foreign-funded enterprises to participate in market competition. Multiple market players are developed and integrated into society to foster a down-top reform path, thus coordinating with the top-down reform path for the national "new normal" and shaping a new situation for reform and development.

References

1. An Yuhong, Economic New Normal, *Macroeconomic Management*, 2014(6).
2. "New" and "Normal" in Xi Jinping's Exposition about "New Normal", www.chinanews.com, August 10, 2014.
3. Xi Jinping Systematically Expounded the "New Normal" for the First Time, Xinhuanet, November 9, 2014.
4. Li Yang, A New Stage in China's Economic Development, *Finance &Trade Economics*, 2013 (11).
5. Shenzhen Bureau of Statistics, Shenzhen Statistical Communiqué on National Economic and Social Development in 2013, April 8, 2014, http://www.sztj.gov.cn/xxgk/tjsj/tjgb/.
6. World Bank, the *World Development Data Manual 2013*, Chinese Financial & Economic Publishing House, 2013.
7. Qiang Guo, Shenzhen, Who Abandoned You, *Zhujiang Economy*, 2002 (12).

Shenzhen-Hong Kong Cooperation: Developmental Course and Overall Review

Tan Gang

Abstract After the developmental course of cooperation between Shenzhen and Hong Kong is summarized, Shenzhen-Hong Kong cooperation is comprehensively evaluated from the perspectives of China's reform and opening up and the East Asian Model, followed by pointing out that Shenzhen-Hong Kong cooperation is the epitome and successful chapter of China's reform and opening up, and its industrial transfer and institutional innovation not only reflect the characteristics of East Asian development but also innovate the East Asian Model, bringing about a new miracle in East Asian development.

Keywords Shenzhen-Hong Kong cooperation · Reform and opening up · East Asian model

The year 2008 was the 30th anniversary of China's reform and opening up and also the 28th anniversary of the establishment of the Shenzhen Special Economic Zone. As indicated by the review of Shenzhen-Hong Kong cooperation, starting from the establishment of the Shenzhen Special Economic Zone, the developmental course of that cooperation almost coincided with China's reform and opening up in time, and involves, in content, various fields of reform and opening up, thus such cooperation better reflects the developmental course of stimulating the reform through the opening up and promoting the opening up through reform; moreover, it has sincerely boosted the sustainable development of both Shenzhen and Hong Kong. To a certain extent, such cooperation has become the epitome of development and a successful chapter of China's reform and opening up. This paper

---

Tan Gang, PhD in Economics, researcher, engaged in research on regional cooperation, especially Shenzhen-Hong Kong cooperation for a long time, Deputy Dean of Shenzhen Institute of Socialism.

T. Gang (✉)
China Development Institute, Shenzhen, Guangdong 518060, China

Y. Yuan (ed.), *Studies on China's Special Economic Zones*, Research Series on the Chinese Dream and China's Development Path,
DOI 10.1007/978-981-10-3704-7_8

summarizes the developmental course of the cooperation between Shenzhen and Hong Kong, and then conducts an overall review of Shenzhen-Hong Kong cooperation, the perspectives of China's reform and opening up and of the East Asian Model.

1 Developmental Course of Shenzhen-Hong Kong Cooperation

Shenzhen-Hong Kong cooperation involves various aspects of Shenzhen and Hong Kong including the economy, society, culture, personnel contacts, cross-border construction and city management. Economic cooperation is the main form and the important motive force for Shenzhen-Hong Kong cooperation. In general, Shenzhen-Hong Kong cooperation is carried out in the following way: Under the "One Country, Two Systems" mode, guided by the comparative interests of Shenzhen and Hong Kong, the transfer of Hong Kong's industries northwards towards Shenzhen serves as the main form and driving force to combine Hong Kong's advantages in capital, market and management with Shenzhen's advantages in location, policy and costs, so as to foster regional economic cooperation which features advantage complementation, labor division and collaboration between Shenzhen and Hong Kong.

With continuous development and gradual intensification over a period of more than 20 years, Shenzhen-Hong Kong economic cooperation, begun in the early 1980s, is broadly divided into three developmental stages: rapid development, relative stagnation and comprehensive promotion.[1] Such cooperation focuses on industrial cooperation, construction and service of cross-border infrastructures, operating mechanisms and policy coordination. The three-stage developmental course of this kind of cooperation is a process of continuously expanding and gradually intensifying at the industrial level, at the city function level and at the institutional level.

[1]Scholars in Guangdong Province and Hong Kong researched the issues concerning the development stages of Shenzhen-Hong Kong cooperation as from the end of 1990s. For example, Tan Gang, Shenzhen-Hong Kong Economic Cooperation Beyond 1997 (Ref. [1]), pp. 470–481; Shao Hanqing, Thinking of How to Embrace A New Situation of Shenzhen-Hong Kong Economic Development, *Hong Kong and Macau Economic Yearbook (2002)*, Hong Kong & Macau Economic Yearbook Press, pp. 335–339; Feng Xiaoyun, Innovations and Breakthroughs in Guangdong, Hong Kong and Macau Economic Cooperation in the New Century, *Hong Kong and Macau Economic Yearbook (2002)*, Hong Kong & Macau Economic Yearbook Press, pp. 301–305; (Ref. [2]), Hong Kong & Macau Research Institute of Development Research Center of the State Council.

(I) **Shenzhen-Hong Kong cooperation is mainly concentrated in the industrial level, and is accompanied by growing economic activities, including trade, investment, consumption, etc.**

The industrial cooperation relationship characterized by the vertical labor division of "Stores in Front and Factories Behind" was established between Shenzhen and Hong Kong in the early 1980s, with the labor-intensive manufacturing industry as the main part of industrial cooperation, proving an ideal space for economic development and economic structural adjustment in both Shenzhen and Hong Kong. At the turn of the century, Shenzhen-Hong Kong industrial cooperation had expanded from the traditional manufacturing industry to high and new technology industries, and the cooperation in the service industry, including finance, logistics and tourism, had also been significantly enhanced. In terms of specific forms of industrial cooperation, Shenzhen and Hong Kong have continuously reinforced and intensified the cooperation in such economic activities as trade, investment, finance and consumption.

First, Hong Kong is always an important import and export partner for Shenzhen and has become the important channel for connecting Shenzhen with countries around the world. In 1995, Shenzhen's direct exports to Hong Kong and Shenzhen's direct imports from Hong Kong were 4.87 billion USD and 1.67 billion USD, accounting for 26.1 and 12.11% of Shenzhen's annual total exports and imports, respectively. The annual average growth rate of Shenzhen-Hong Kong trade has markedly accelerated since Hong Kong's return to the motherland. It was further intensified after the implementation of the CEPA in 2004. The annual total trade in goods between Shenzhen's ports and Hong Kong reached 47.3 billion USD in 2005 (see Table 1).

Second, Hong Kong has always been the most important foreign capital source for Shenzhen, while Shenzhen has established overseas enterprises mainly in Hong Kong. According to statistics, the actual cumulative amount of Hong Kong's investments in Shenzhen amounted to 7.64 billion USD from 1979 to 1996, accounting for 66% of the actual investments made by foreign investors in Shenzhen; although the proportion of Hong Kong's investments in foreign investments actually used in Shenzhen decreased somewhat, it still exceeded 50% in 1997. Hong Kong's investments used in agreements and actually used were 6654 million yuan and 6089 million yuan, respectively in 2007, making up about 60%.

The growth rate of Hong Kong's actual investments in Shenzhen reached 21.5% during the period 1987–1994, declined to 9.1% during the period 1995–2001 and

Table 1 The growth of the Shenzhen-Hong Kong trade volume since 1997 (unit: 100 million USD)

	1997	2000	2003	2004	2005	2006
Import volume	12.4	16.1	20.3	24.6	23.1	18.5
Export volume	72.3	113.7	263.7	341.7	450.6	581.4
Total import and export volume	84.7	129.8	284.0	366.3	473.7	599.9

Source Shenzhen Bureau of Trade and Industry

Table 2 Changes in the growth rate of Hong Kong's investments actually used in Shenzhen

Period	Growth rate of Hong Kong's investments actually used in Shenzhen %
1987–1994	21.51
1995–2001	9.1
1997–2003	8.1
2004–2006	10.98

Source Data from *Shenzhen Statistical Yearbook* over the years

slightly rose to 10.98% during the period 2004–2006 (see Table 2). At present, 70% of foreign investments in Shenzhen come from Hong Kong, and more than 10,000 Hong Kong-funded enterprises have been established in Shenzhen, accounting for more than 70% of all foreign-funded enterprises in Shenzhen.

On the other hand, Shenzhen has also actively taken advantage of Hong Kong in order to enter the world market. At the end of the Twentieth century, 69 among the 153 overseas enterprises established by Shenzhen were present in Hong Kong, accounting for 45% of all overseas enterprises established by Shenzhen. In 2004 and 2005, 15 and 24 of Shenzhen's enterprises were newly-established in Hong Kong, the agreement-based investments were 184 million and 213 million USD, respectively, and the actual investments were 126 million and 44 million USD, respectively. Twenty enterprises were newly set up in the period January—August, 2006, with a substantial increase in the amount of investments.

Third, Shenzhen-Hong Kong financial cooperation has been steadily promoted. Before and after Hong Kong's return to the motherland, Shenzhen became the main area for the flow of Hong Kong dollars onto the Chinese Mainland, accounting for about 75 and 30% of the total inflow to the Chinese Mainland and Hong Kong dollar supply, respectively. Actually, there was a limited circulation of Hong Kong dollars in Shenzhen. Hong Kong dollar and US dollar two-way clearing arrangements and the networking of a real-time payment settlement system were initiated between Shenzhen and Hong Kong in 1998. Since then, the used amount has continuously increased and the daily turnover through joint clearing arrangements rose from 25 million equivalent Hong Kong dollars in the first half of 1998 to 137 million equivalent Hong Kong dollars in June, 2006, and the daily turnover through the networking of the real-time payment settlement system soared from about 50 million equivalent Hong Kong dollars to 737 million equivalent Hong Kong dollars in the same period. The total amount of transactions processed through the two-way real-time payment system exceeded 113 billion and 150 billion equivalent Hong Kong dollars in 2004 and 2005, respectively. Currently, Hong Kong's banks have established 14 branches on the Chinese Mainland, 10 of which are present in Shenzhen, accounting for as high as 71%, including 6 banks established after the implementation of CEPA in 2004, making up 75% of the foreign banking institutions established in Shenzhen in the same period. Moreover, intensified cooperation between Shenzhen and Hong Kong and the increase in consumption and house purchases by Hong Kong residents in Shenzhen have also objectively pushed forward the financial business in Shenzhen and Hong Kong. According to statistics, at the end of 2005, the total individual consumer credit at Hong Kong banks amounted to 0.48 billion USD, accounting for 93% of the total individual consumer credit at foreign banks in Shenzhen (0.52 billion USD).

(II) **Shenzhen and Hong Kong have engaged in active cooperation at city level, with more and more cooperative projects carried out, including city functions, cross-border infrastructure construction and cross-border services**

With the intensification of industrial cooperation between Shenzhen and Hong Kong, the construction of major cross-border infrastructure projects represented by the port construction, Shenzhen River control and improvement, Western channel investments have been initiated between Shenzhen and Hong Kong, offering convenient and efficient cross-border city facilities for Shenzhen-Hong Kong cooperation. Meanwhile, city developmental strategies, respectively developed by Shenzhen and Hong Kong, in particular, the City Development Strategy 2030 developed in recent years, have laid a good foundation for the connection of city functions between Shenzhen and Hong Kong. Presently, an extensive, multi-channel port connection has been built between Shenzhen and Hong Kong, and the construction and connection of cross-border infrastructures, including transport, energy and communications, has also been enlarged. As a result, Shenzhen has basically developed the conditions, concerning the city functions, for complementing the functions of Hong Kong as an international financial, trade, shipping and information center.

With an increasingly intense flow of people and materials between Shenzhen and Hong Kong, not only has Shenzhen become the busiest port city nationwide, but Shenzhen and Hong Kong have also become the most important channel for connecting China with the world's economy. In 1996, the inbound and outbound tourists through Shenzhen's ports reached 63.20 million person-times, accounting for more than 50% of the national total of inbound and outbound tourists, ranking No. 1 nationwide for many consecutive years; the inbound and outbound vehicles were 8.53 million vehicle-times, accounting for 75% of the national total. In 2005, the people entering and leaving the Chinese Mainland through the first-line ports at Shenzhen reached 159 million person-times, accounting for more than 50% of the national total. The inbound and outbound transport means were 14.94 million vehicles (ship)-times, accounting for about 75% of the national total every year. According to a relevant survey, currently, about 200,000 people go through Luohu Port, on average, every day, nearly 70% of whom choose Shenzhen as their first destination.

Since the 1980s when the cooperation between Hong Kong and the Chinese Mainland, in particular Shenzhen, began, besides sightseeing tours on the Chinese Mainland, Hong Kong residents have also gradually gone north for investing, carrying on business, shopping, even residing, while Shenzhen has always been an important city for Hong Kong residents going northward to consume, especially after Hong Kong's return to the motherland (see Table 3).

As the city mutual relationship of dependence between Shenzhen and Hong Kong has become closer in supply of fresh and live products, water and power

Table 3 The proportion of consumption by Hong Kong residents in Shenzhen in their northward movement to consume (%)

Year	Based on consumption person-time				Based on consumption amount		
	Guangdong province (%)	Shenzhen (%)	Outside Guangdong province (%)	Total (%)	Guangdong province (%)	Outside Guangdong province (%)	Total (%)
2001	93.0	45.7	7.0	100.0	71.0	29.0	100.0
2002	93.8	45.3	6.5	100.3	73.4	26.6	100.0
2003	94.1	48.2	5.9	100.0	75.0	25.0	100.0
2004	94.0	48.2	6.0	100.0	71.3	28.8	100.0

Source Census and Statistics Department, Hong Kong SAR Government

supply, trans-regional living and tourism, cross-border services have emerged and are constantly advancing, laying a good social foundation for further connection between Shenzhen and Hong Kong. With expanding contacts and exchanges between Shenzhen and Hong Kong, thanks to similarities in their life styles and living conditions, more and more Hong Kong residents have purchased houses and live? in Shenzhen. As shown by a relevant survey, the houses sold externally in Shenzhen have accounted for about 10% in recent years and more than 70% of Hong Kong residents involved in the survey were willing to buy houses in Shenzhen, while more than 60% of Hong Kong residents have fallen in love with this life style: working in Hong Kong but living in Shenzhen.

(III) **Shenzhen-Hong Kong cooperation has gradually extended to the institutional level, with an intensification of cooperation regarding the operating mechanism, management system, etc.**

Against the background of growing integration between Hong Kong and the Chinese Mainland,[2] as Shenzhen-Hong Kong cross-border economic activities and cooperation fields are increasing, Shenzhen and Hong Kong have also dovetailed and cooperated with each other in economic operational mechanisms, management systems and city governance, and the institutional cooperation has become an important form of the economic relationship between Hong Kong and the Chinese Mainland, including Shenzhen.[3] Shenzhen has extensively drawn upon the Hong Kong Experience and the Hong Kong Model in the establishment of market operation mechanisms, operations based on international practice, the improvement of the market system and urban area management; Shenzhen has even developed many behaviors and concepts which adapt to Hong Kong. This not only is an important content of the institutional cooperation between Shenzhen and Hong Kong at the

[2]Yang Ruwan, The Process of Integration Between Hong Kong and the Chinese Mainland during the period 1997–2007, (Ref. [3]), pp. 30–34.

[3]Yuan Yiming, Institutional Cooperation—Future Forms of Economic Relations Between Hong Kong and the Chinese Mainland, (Ref. [3]), pp. 269–274.

initial stage, but it has also laid an extensive social foundation for subsequent cooperation in the operating mechanisms between Shenzhen and Hong Kong.

In the new century, especially with the signing and implementation of CEPA (2003), Shenzhen-Hong Kong Cooperation "1+8" Agreement (2004), "1+6" Agreement (2007) and other documents, Shenzhen-Hong Kong cooperation has been elevated from a non-governmental level to a governmental level, and Shenzhen-Hong Kong cooperation mechanisms have been gradually established and improved; furthermore, both Shenzhen and Hong Kong have expanded the fields of cooperation to institutional arrangements and mechanism improvements, with an obvious increase in the level of cooperation, thus Shenzhen-Hong Kong cooperation has entered a new developmental period.

Clearly, the smooth accession of the Chinese Mainland to the WTO has presented new challenges and opportunities for Shenzhen-Hong Kong economic cooperation which had been promoted for more than 20 years and had yielded great achievements, that is, how to push forward the bilateral cooperation consistent with the WTO basic rules on the basis of "One Country, Two Systems" and make it meet the basic requirements of "One Country, Two Systems" and adapt to WTO rules while dovetailing bilateral cooperation which had been conducted or was underway.

As the Chinese Mainland-Hong Kong Closer Economic Partnership Arrangement (CEPA)[4] took effect in 2004 and has been promoted by stages, CEPA has also exerted an important impact on Shenzhen-Hong Kong economic cooperation, it has greatly expanded the scope and fields of cooperation between them and has enabled a substantive expansion in the depth of cooperation. The cooperation model based on international rules has also been adopted to ensure a deep and wide cooperation between Shenzhen and Hong Kong at the institutional level.

With the implementation of the Pan-Pearl River Delta Regional Cooperation Agreement 2004 ("9+2") and the emergence of the Pan-Pearl River Delta Economic Region,[5] it is particularly urgent for Shenzhen and Hong Kong, as the heartland of the Pan-Pearl River Delta, to seize great opportunities from regional cooperation, comprehensively innovate the Shenzhen-Hong Kong cooperation advantages, join hands to make expansion, give play to the role of the regional hub platform, go beyond their own economic regional boundary constraints to jointly find a new space for growth and development base, and stretch out along the broad spaces of the Pan-Pearl River Delta.

The "1+8" Agreement and the "1+6" Agreement signed between Shenzhen and Hong Kong in 2004 and 2007, respectively[6] represented an important step forward

[4]Economic integration between Hong Kong and the Chinese Mainland accelerated, http://finance.sina.com.cn/nz/CEPA/index.shtml.

[5]Innovative cooperation in the Pan-pearl River Delta Region, "9+2" economic base circle, http://gd.news.sina.com.cn/spt/fanzhusanjiao/.

[6]For "1+8" Agreement, see Hong Kong SAR Government: Shenzhen-Hong Kong Cooperation is Not Hotly? by Only One Side, "1+8" Agreement was Signed, http://www.southcn.com/news/gdnews/gdtodayimportant/200406180173.htm; for "1+6" Agreement, see Shenzhen and Hong Kong Signed "1+6" Agreement, Ushering in a New Era for Cooperation, http://gd.sohu.com/20071219/n254175783.shtml.

for Shenzhen-Hong Kong cooperation within the CEPA and Guangdong-Hong Kong cooperation framework. Both agreements involved extensive fields of Shenzhen-Hong Kong cooperation and specific measures, and were highly forward-looking and groundbreaking, and this indicated that the bilateral cooperation had entered a new stage of a higher level, wider fields and larger space. Merely in terms of innovation of the cooperation mechanism, both agreements specially expounded Shenzhen-Hong Kong cooperation mechanisms and stressed that both sides could conduct in-depth discussions about cooperation contents concerning the two cities under the Guangdong-Hong Kong cooperation framework. Actually, that went beyond some long-standing boundaries in bilateral cooperation, and it especially removed the status inequality in cooperation and dialogue between Shenzhen and Hong Kong, thus opening up a new path for both sides to establish a direct dialogue platform and cooperation mechanisms, conducive to innovating the Shenzhen-Hong Kong cooperation mechanism. For example, at the end of October, 2006, the Standing Committee of the National People's Congress adopted the decision to authorize the Hong Kong Special Administrative Region to exercise jurisdiction over the Hong Kong side of the Shenzhen Bay Port, resulting in "two inspections at one place", thus breaking through the administrative and judicial barriers between Shenzhen and Hong Kong, creating a new cooperative mode between the two governments. In mid-May, 2007, both governments signed the "Shenzhen-Hong Kong Innovation Circle" Cooperation Agreement. It can be deemed as elevated to a national strategy, to some extent, because it was recognized by the Ministry of Science and Technology. Of course, it will greatly promote bilateral cooperation. We have full reason to expect that the establishment and improvement of Shenzhen-Hong Kong cooperation mechanisms will be beneficial to breaking the cooperation bottlenecks under the new situation to further increase the level of bilateral cooperation, and expand the cooperative fields in order to promote the prosperity and development of Shenzhen and Hong Kong.

2 Overall Review of Shenzhen-Hong Kong Cooperation

(I) Shenzhen-Hong Kong cooperation is the epitome of development and a successful chapter in China's reform and opening up

More than 30 years have elapsed since China initiated the reform and opening up in 1978. When it comes to the institutional reform which started in rural areas and then advanced to cities or the opening up which was first initiated in the special economic zones and then gradually extended nationwide in the developmental course of China's reform and opening up, it mostly originated from the areas or fields less subject to the traditional planned economic system. As the opening up gave rise to reform and the reform was intensified to promote the opening up, tremendous achievements were made in the reform and opening-up pilot areas, represented by the Shenzhen Special Economic Zone. As a product of reform and opening up, Shenzhen-Hong Kong cooperation has better given play to the important roles of "Hong Kong factors" and "Chinese Mainland factors" (including "Shenzhen factors") to greatly boost bilateral economic development. Concerning Shenzhen, Shenzhen-Hong Kong cooperation has played an important role in the course of the reform and the opening up of the Shenzhen Special Economic Zone and has become an important driving force and choice of path towards industrialization, urbanization and modernization (Ref. [4]).

From the perspective of China's reform and the opening up, Shenzhen-Hong Kong cooperation has benefited from the trend of the times of China's reform and opening up, and the huge opportunities from international industrial adjustment and transfer. Thus it had distinct characteristics from the beginning: carrying out reform and innovation, opening up towards foreign countries, enlivening the domestic economy, finding a developmental path—stimulating reform through the opening up, promoting the opening up through reform.

Thanks to a bold experimentation and the first breakthrough in Shenzhen-Hong Kong cooperation, Shenzhen has become the first to enter the international market with Hong Kong as a relay station, develop an outward-looking economic system, become an important area and force for national reform and opening up. Shenzhen can closely, intuitively draw upon and learn from Hong Kong's successful experience, adopt the international practices and rules available in Hong Kong to build a relatively complete framework system of a socialist market economy. In the process of Shenzhen-Hong Kong economic cooperation, Shenzhen has gradually fostered the main spirit—reform, innovation and opening up as the root, source and soul of the special zones, highlighting the spirit of the times: reform and innovation.

Moreover, the important significance of Shenzhen-Hong Kong cooperation for the industrialization, modernization and urbanization of contemporary China should also be fully recognized. From a global perspective, before the opening up, reform and innovation occurred on the Chinese Mainland, industrialization and modernization in four areas—the Chinese Mainland, Hong Kong, Taiwan and Macau—were basically independently carried out and promoted. After the reform and opening up policy was implemented on the Chinese Mainland, inspiringly, originally independent modernization and industrialization merged and mutually advanced, starting from Shenzhen-Hong Kong cooperation, among these four areas, especially among Hong Kong, Macau, Taiwan and the Chinese Mainland. In other words, Shenzhen-Hong Kong cooperation also kicked off the integration of these four areas in China, showing an outstanding feature—driving the integration and common progress of four large areas in China, thus really initiating the industrialization and modernization process across the whole of China.

Therefore, in this sense, we have full reason to recognize that Shenzhen-Hong Kong economic cooperation has become the prominent mark and epitome of the reform, opening up and modernization in contemporary China. In the big wave of China's reform and opening up, with the successful practice of Shenzhen-Hong Kong economic cooperation, Hong Kong and Shenzhen have worked together to write a brand-new chapter and play a successful role in that wave.

(II) Industrial development and institutional innovation: The East Asian Model characteristics of Shenzhen-Hong Kong cooperation and its innovations

The East Asian Economic Miracle marked by rapid economic growth encompasses high-speed economic growth and industrialization in East Asian countries or territories, such as the rapid development of Japan in the 1960s, the rise of the Four Asian Tigers in the 1970s, the takeoff of ASEAN and South China since the 1980s. According to an analysis of the rapidly growing East Asian economy, although there is not a single East Asian developmental model, different policies indeed shared many similarities, and a series of common policies beneficial to the development of a market economy were implemented to promote high accumulation and more rational allocation of resources and thus give birth to the East Asian Economic Miracle, thus constituting the East Asian Model.[7]

From the perspective of the similarities and fundamental characteristics of East Asian countries or territories, the East Asian Model can be summarized as follows[8]: (1) Based on the complementation of a regional economy and a system of regional division, induced and pulled by spread effects and backwash effects, a multi-tier, gradient, transfer type industrial division and transfer developmental mechanism took shape, accelerating regional industrial circulation in East Asia and bringing more East Asian countries and territories into the system of international division, as a result, this maintained and unceasingly enhanced the vitality of East Asian economy and promoted sustained evolution of the East Asian Economic Miracle. (2) Governments rationally conducted institutional innovations and adopted government substitution modes to directly nurture and expand the market, thus developing the developmental strategies, policies and measures conducive to economic growth. According to the World Bank, this mainly covers the following aspects: rationally choose the export-oriented developmental strategy; take the industrial policy for supporting key elements and boosting upgrading; keep high savings and investments focused on effectively allocating resources and improving labor productivity, and adopt the basic economic policy for utilizing foreign capital and absorbing foreign advanced technologies; carry out the macroeconomic management policy for ensuring stable economic operations, combining government guidance with market regulation, placing equal emphasis on growth and equity.

As analyzed from the perspective of the East Asian Economic Miracle and the East Asian Model, Shenzhen-Hong Kong cooperation reflects the developmental

---

[7]For classical exposition about the East Asian Miracle and the East Asian Model, see the World Bank: *The East Asian Miracle: Economic Growth and Public Policy*, Chinese Financial & Economic Publishing House, 1995.

[8](Japan) Ohashi Hideo, *Formation of the Regional Economic Circle in East Asia and the Roles of Japan*, Ma Hong, (Japan) Shinyasu Hoshino ed.: *The Economic Developmental Direction for South China and the Outlook on the Economic Relations of Hong Kong, Taiwan and Japan*; Shenzhen, Haitian Publishing House, 1995, p. 310.

characteristics of East Asia and also represents an innovation and exploration of the East Asian Model to some extent (Ref. [5]).

First, initially driven by and focused on industrial transfer and absorption, Shenzhen-Hong Kong economic cooperation embodies the industrial division and transfer development mechanism of the East Asian Model—becoming the initial form and path towards the opening-up of China's special economic zones to a certain degree, and such cooperation has enabled beneficial experimentation and innovation of the implementation mode, resulting in a new industrial cooperative mode characterized by a regional industrial chain. According to research, the industrial transfer in Shenzhen-Hong Kong cooperation basically follows "the flying-geese structure" developmental path characteristic of the industrial evolution in the East Asian Model, and shows the economic cooperation pattern represented by the vertical labor division called "Stores in Front and Factories Behind" to promote bilateral industrial cooperation.

Second, Shenzhen-Hong Kong cooperation characterized by institutional innovations is the product of China's institutional reform and opening up. Shenzhen-Hong Kong economic cooperation based on One Country, Two Systems is the outcome of institutional innovations. Shenzhen-Hong Kong cooperation is impossible without reform and opening up. Meanwhile, actually, for Shenzhen, both industrial cooperation and the dovetailing of the operating mechanism also involve the process of institutional innovations. Thanks to government-led reform and innovations of the market system, market mechanism and market regulation, direct involvement in market formation and operation, and innovations of the institutional mode, Shenzhen has become the first to preliminarily establish a government-regulated market economic system nationwide.

Third, Shenzhen-Hong Kong cooperation, boosted by institutional innovations, has also effectively innovated the East Asian Model, especially in industrial cooperation, it has extended from "Stores in Front and Factories Behind" cooperation to joint construction of the regional industrial chain, bringing about innovations to the East Asian Model. As revealed by the course of Shenzhen-Hong Kong industrial cooperation, the traditional Shenzhen-Hong Kong cooperation mode—"Stores in Front and Factories Behind"—has faced huge challenges since the mid and late 1990s, putting bilateral cooperation in trouble to some extent. On the one hand, Hong Kong's economy slowed down, and even stagnated, no technology-intensive industries were available for support, and it was difficult for the service industry with comparative advantages to fully enter Shenzhen, making it difficult for continuously pushing ahead with industrial transfer based on the flying-geese model; on the other hand, with sustained rapid development of Shenzhen's economy, high and new technology industries were growing and became pillar industries, while the costs for doing business in Shenzhen gradually rose, the access threshold and standard for Hong Kong's low-end industries increased; as a result, Hong Kong-funded enterprises originally giving priority to efficiency shifted to other areas with more comparative advantages, while Hong Kong's productive service industry with comparative advantages could not be smoothly introduced due to institutional arrangements. In the Twenty-first century, especially with institutional innovations and arrangements including CEPA, "1+8" and "1+6", both sides have gradually gotten out of the standstill of industrial cooperation under the flying-geese structure in recent years. Both sides have established step by step new comparative advantages to shape a new situation of industrial chain allocation between Shenzhen and Hong Kong on the basis of comparative advantages, thus two-way industrial transfer and absorption has occurred between Shenzhen and Hong Kong, and the original single, one-way vertical industrial division mode in bilateral industrial cooperation has been changed. A shift from "Stores in Front and Factories Behind" to a regional industrial chain is an outstanding innovation of the East Asian Model (especially the flying-geese structure) made by Shenzhen-Hong Kong cooperation.

(III) Shenzhen-Hong Kong cooperation has effectively stimulated the sustainable economic and social development of Shenzhen and Hong Kong

Overall, Shenzhen-Hong Kong cooperation is one of the important and successful ways for achieving sustained rapid economic and social development in Shenzhen, and such cooperation has also promoted the continuous development of Hong Kong since the 1980s, thus Shenzhen-Hong Kong cooperation has delivered a remarkable performance to the economic and social development in Shenzhen and Hong Kong (see Table 4).

According to a metrical study finding obtained by one of Shenzhen's scholars (Ref. [6]), the performance of Shenzhen-Hong Kong cooperation was obviously higher than that of the cooperation between Guangdong Province and Hong Kong, between the Chinese Mainland and Hong Kong (see Table 5). As shown by data in this table, as Shenzhen-Hong Kong cooperation intensified by each 1%, per-capita output in Shenzhen grew by 0.87%, higher than that (0.73, 0.39%) in Guangdong Province and on the Chinese Mainland in the case of the cooperation between Guangdong Province and Hong Kong, between the Chinese Mainland and Hong Kong. This indicates that the actual performance of cooperation between Shenzhen and Hong Kong, between Guangdong Province and Hong Kong, between the Chinese Mainland and Hong Kong decreases with the increasing distance of regional connection, which is highly consistent with the situation of regional extension in the economic integration between Hong Kong and the Chinese Mainland: the closer an area is to Hong Kong, the higher the integration is with Hong Kong's economy, and the more salient the economic growth effect of bilateral cooperation is on that area.

In view of the trend of economic development in the contemporary world, Shenzhen-Hong Kong economic cooperation reflects the characteristics of international industrial transfer based on the opening up and is also closely related to institutional innovations mainly characterized by institutional reform, thus such

Table 4 Economic growth of Shenzhen and Hong Kong since the Shenzhen-Hong Kong cooperation

Year	Hong Kong (100 million Hong Kong dollars)	Shenzhen (100 million yuan)	Shenzhen: Hong Kong
1979	3994	1.96	1:2037
1980	4408	2.7	1:1633
1985	5822	39	1:149
1990	8455	172	1:49
1995	11,100	796	1:14
1997	12,161	1130	1:10
2000	13,148	1665	1:7.9
2004	15,099	4282	1:3.5
2005	16,234	4927	1:3.3
2006	17,359	5884	1:3.0
2007	18,400	6765	1:2.7

Note (1) To simplify, 1:1 is taken as the ratio between both places, without considering the actual exchange rate. If the exchange rate is considered, the ratio between both places in 1979 and 2007 was approximately 1:549 and 1:2.7, respectively. (2) Data come from the statistical yearbooks of both places. 2007 Hong Kong data are estimated according to an annual growth rate of 6% predicted by the Hong Kong SAR Government, while 2007 Shenzhen data are those released by the Shenzhen Bureau of Statistics at the end of January, 2008

Table 5 Comparisons regarding the performance of cooperation between Shenzhen and Hong Kong, between Guangdong Province and Hong Kong, between the Chinese Mainland and Hong Kong

	As Shenzhen-Hong Kong cooperation intensified by each 1%	As Guangdong-Hong Kong cooperation intensified by each 1%	As Chinese Mainland-Hong Kong cooperation intensified by each 1%
Per-capita output growth %	0.87% (Shenzhen)	0.73% (Guangdong)	0.39% (Chinese Mainland)

Note This table is based on the calculations in (Ref. [6])

cooperation can deliver an excellent performance. This shows that as the epitome of China's reform and opening up, Shenzhen-Hong Kong economic cooperation has naturally become the integral part of the East Asian Economic Miracle since the 1980s and the main carrier of the East Asian Model and the East Asian Miracle, and it has successfully extended, to this day, the East Asian Economic Miracle which started in the 1950s. With the sustained rapid growth of Shenzhen as an urban economic system, we have full reason to believe that Shenzhen-Hong Kong cooperation has extended the East Asian Miracle and elevated it to a new height; Shenzhen and Hong Kong have worked together to create a new miracle in East Asian economy.

References

1. Li Luoli, Tan Gang et al., *Prosperity or Decline*, Hong Kong Xidi Commercial Publishing Co., Ltd., 1999.
2. Tan Gang, Shenzhen-Hong Kong Cooperation: Developmental Course and Overall Objective, H*ong Kong and Macao Research*, Autumn, 2007.
3. Jiang Tanyu, *Retrospect and Prospects for the Ten Years after the Return of Hong Kong*, China Review Academic Publishers Limited, 2007.
4. Tan Gang, Jointly Creating Prosperity—Review of Shenzhen-Hong Kong Economic Cooperation, *Practice and Theory of SEZs*, 2006(1).
5. Tan Gang, On the International Significance of Shenzhen-Hong Kong Economic Cooperation, *Theory and Practice of SEZs*, 1998(8).
6. Chen Xiuzhen, A Metrical Study of the Economic Growth Effect of Economic Integration between Hong Kong and the Chinese Mainland, *China Opening Journal,* 2005(5).

Selection of the Direction of the Developmental Path for China's Special Economic Zones in the New Period

Zhou Yunyuan

Concurrently discussing the building of the Shenzhen-Hong Kong-Zhuhai-Macau Free Trade Zone

Abstract This paper holds that, with construction and development for nearly 30 years, the special economic zones with Chinese characteristics are the pilot areas that were given the first priority for developing in the reform and the opening up and that they are also the famous brands for China to better participate in the integration of the world economy in the 21st century. The special economic zones are the special products of China's reform and opening up. According to the developmental philosophy of keeping pace with the times, it is inevitably necessary to achieve the transformation of the special economic zones after China's 30-year-long reform and opening up. We should proceed from the actual development of productive forces and their future developmental trends in China's special economic zones, reposition the special economic zones and substitute new functions so as to develop them into free trade zones and free ports in a classified way in due time.

Keywords Reform and opening up · China's special economic zones · Direction of the developmental path

Zhou Yunyuan, (1952—), Professor of Economics, at Sun Yat-Sen University; this paper bases its analysis only on the first batch of four special economic zones established in China, and does not include the Hainan and Pudong New Area, which was established later.

Z. Yunyuan (✉)
The Center for Studies on the Hong Kong, Macau and Pearl River Delta, Sun Yat-Sen University, Guangzhou, Guangdong 510275, China

Y. Yuan (ed.), *Studies on China's Special Economic Zones*, Research Series on the Chinese Dream and China's Development Path,
DOI 10.1007/978-981-10-3704-7_9

1 Opportunities and Challenges for China's Special Economic Zones in the New Period

(I) China's all-round, deep involvement in the developmental pattern of the world's economic integration

After many years of WTO negotiations, China joined the WTO as a developing country at the end of 2001, which undoubtedly added new vitality to the WTO. In the process of increasing regionalization and integration of the global economy, the economic development of various countries and territories is required to be carried out in a standardized way subject to the regulations and rules of relevant international organizations including the WTO. Since the 21st century, generally, the special economic zones in the world, important for a sustained development of the global economy are still playing a very important role amid the integration and regionalization of the world's economy. Without doubt, some specific functions of the special zones have changed, especially their considerable expansion, which is still continuing in the field of free trade. For example, the ASEAN Free Trade Area is continuously expanding and developing, the ASEAN 10+3 (ASEAN 10 countries plus China, Japan and South Korea) mechanism has been fixed in agreements and is gradually advancing, and new free trade areas are also being built in the new period; for example, 34 countries from South America, North America and the Caribbean Region (a population of 0.8 billion) have also signed agreements to establish the Free Trade Area of the Americas. To some extent, this shows that the free trade area is still a very important form for the development of today's world economy. China's special economic zones were established and developed by drawing upon the beneficial experience in expanding special economic zones in the world during the reform and the opening up; therefore, in face of the new developmental pattern of today's world economy, it is necessary for China's special economic zones to seize the situation, implement the developmental strategy in line with the times, reposition themselves in due time, transform their own functions to gradually move towards the economic developmental model which fits in with China's actual conditions and the developmental trend of the world's economy.

(II) Opportunities and challenges for China in the all-round opening up in the new period

Since the 1990s, China has further expanded the outward-looking economy and pressed ahead with all-round reform and opening up, especially the development and construction of the central and western regions have upgraded China's profound opening up to a new height. Since the 21st century, China has speeded up its all-directional, multi-layered and wide-ranging opening up. Under such a developmental pattern, the special economic zones are no longer the only areas for the opening up in China and are not the areas which exclusively enjoyed special policies in the past; instead, they are required to participate in the global labor division and cooperation to develop and enhance their own economic and social strength as China is, on the whole, integrating into the regionalization and integration of the world's economy. The driving force resulting from competition and development in the hinterland has also, to a certain extent, compelled the special economic zones to make their own improvement and develop themselves according to higher requirements. There is a prevailing view—hinterland-like development occurs in special zones. Although this view is one-sided, the reality is that if the special zones show a hinterland-like development, they will be devitalized and cannot achieve a sustainable development for a longer time. The special economic zones should conform to the developmental trend of the world's economy, and make the most of their originally developed advantages and potential, the solid foundation built during the nearly 30 years in order to continue carrying forward the pragmatic spirit of forging ahead amidst the changing international market, learn better and draw upon the successful models from international economic development, seek out the developmental model for further development, which is unquestionably the key to the future development of the special economic zones in the new period.

2 Selection of the Direction of the Future Developmental Path for China's Special Economic Zones

The construction and development of China's special economic zones have been going on for more than 30 years, since August 26, 1980 when the Regulations of Guangdong Province on the Special Economic Zones was passed during the 15th Session of the Standing Committee of the 5th National People's Congress. However, seminars on the direction of the developmental path for the special economic zones have been held many times in this period. This is the inevitable outcome of the development of China's special economic zones because the special economic zones were special new things arising from China's reform and opening up; when they were in the crucial historical developmental period, the developmental trend of the special economic zones first aroused the people's attention and discussions. What mode will be adopted for developing the special economic zones with Chinese characteristics in the new historical period naturally becomes the hot topic in our discussions.

(I) Discussions about the direction of the future developmental path for China's special economic zones

At the beginning of the 21st century, Professor Su Dongbin from Shenzhen University said: "As the human being is embracing the new century, the special zones are young," and believed that "only when the basic framework of the market economic system takes shape nationwide, does the mission of China's special economic zones as "special zones" end. Even so, as "non-special zones" in the future, China's special economic zones may also make special contributions to China and to mankind."[1]

As early as 1995 when the construction and development of China's special economic zones had been going on for 15 years and there was an important issue concerning how to continue developing China's special economic zones, in order to discuss how to identify new developmental goals for the special economic zones according to international practices under the new situation and find a new development and mode, the United Nations Development Programme and the China Institute for Reform and Development jointly held an international seminar in Haikou City on April 13–14, 1995, whose theme was "What Course to Follow for China's Special Economic Zones". Nearly 100 experts and scholars from home and abroad attended that seminar. In light of the construction and development of China's special economic zones of that time, and their future historical mission, when delivering his speech, the author pointed out, "We should seize the situation to develop the special economic zones in a classified way, and turn some of them into free trade areas, some of them into free ports in the future." Such a view aroused the interest from part of the scholars present at that seminar. (The full text of my speech was published in *Shenzhen Special Zone Daily* (Theory column) on June 28, 1995, while the main views from my speech were summed up in the *Hainan Daily* on July 8.) In order to celebrate the 20th anniversary of the establishment of China's special economic zones, the Development Research Center of the State Council, Shenzhen, Hainan, Xiamen, Zhuhai, Shantou Special Economic Zones and the Pudong New Area of Shanghai jointly held a theoretical seminar on the "Special Economic Zones and the Building of Socialism with Chinese Characteristics" in Shenzhen on September 12–14, 2000. Some experts believed that "after the market economy is established and universal policies are implemented, the original mission of the special zones will be finished in substance rather than in form, unless the Central Government gives a new mission to the special zones, for example, developing them into international special zones such as "trade areas" or "free ports"." (See the articles written by Min Xun et al., *Xinhua Digest*, 2000 [1]). In the seminar on the 25th anniversary of the establishment of the special economic zones, some experts held that the "special economic zones should continue serving as experimental fields, demonstration areas and pacesetters, carrying out the outlook on scientific development for the whole country, gathering and offering fresh experience for building a harmonious socialist society."

In an overall review of the development of the special economic zones around the world in 2006, Professor Zhong Jian believed that there were five types of special economic zones in the world, including trade-oriented special economic zones, industry and trade-oriented special economic zones, technology-focused special economic zones, integrated special economic zones and cross-border special economic zones. He also thought that China's special economic zones were

[1]Su Dongbin, *Special Frontier Topics Concerning China's Special Economic Zones*, China Economic Publishing House, July, 2000, the 1st Edition.

integrated, multifunctional special economic zones. Of course, the special zones developed differently due to varied geographical, economic and social conditions; for example, Shenzhen and Zhuhai mainly focused on industry with a concurrent development of commerce, tourism, real estate, agriculture, animal husbandry and fishing; Xiamen was a seaport-based special economic zone, dominated by industry, where commerce and tourism were concurrently developed and some free port policies were implemented; Shantou Special Economic Zone was between both the above special economic zones, and had the industrial and agricultural characteristics of Shenzhen and Zhuhai and the port foreign trade characteristics of Xiamen.[2] The regionalization and integration of today's world economic development is irresistible; expanding a multi-tier, wide-ranging free trade area and free port mode is undoubtedly very important for such regionalization and integration, and such a mode has been proved to be an effective economic developmental model by the way that the world economic development has unfolded. The 21st century is a new period of cooperation and development—a period full of opportunities and competition, during which realizing the great rejuvenation of the Chinese nation will be of inestimable historical significance. As this history developed up to the end of 2008, in the working conference on special economic zones on November 18 and 19 of that year, the developmental goals for the new period with respect to the three special economic zones of Guangdong Province were specified: "Shenzhen will see the building of a brand-new public service-oriented government in 2013", "Zhuhai will become a new ecologically civilized special zone" and "Shantou will be turned into a modern, multifunctional, integrated outward-looking port city." At China's Special Economic Zones Forum 2008 organized by the China Center for Special Economic Zone Research of Shenzhen University, Professor Zhong Jian still insisted on and expounded the five modes put forward in 2006 for the development of the special economic zones around the world, and believed that the special economic zones would still enjoy a very large developmental space in China in the future.[3] Some experts held that the special economic zones should have first implementation and experimentation in more fields and more aspects, especially the economic system, social system, administrative and political system, the relationship between people and society, and continue serving as the windows and experimental fields for driving China's reform and development forward. In the future, areas like Shenzhen can play a bigger role and continue providing the whole country with fresh experience and practices, new strategic ways of thinking and new modes of thinking. There is still a long time before the special zones become outmoded, thus the special zones should endure and act as the experimental fields for a long time in the whole process of China's reform and development. (See *Shenzhen Special Zone Daily*, December 22, 2008). The Reform and Developmental Plan for the Pearl River Delta Region approved by the State Council

---

[2]Jian [1], pp. 14–16, 400.

[3]China Center for Special Economic Zone Research, Shenzhen University, *Selected Papers of Seminar on the 30th Anniversary of Reform and Opening Up*, 2008, pp. 9–10.

at the end of 2008 specified a new functional positioning for Shenzhen and Zhuhai situated in the Pearl River Delta. According to that Plan, Shenzhen City should continue playing the roles of a special economic zone as a window, experimental field and demonstration area, enhance scientific and technological research and development, high-end service functions, reinforce its position as a national central economic city and national innovation-oriented city, and become a model city for socialism with Chinese characteristics and an international city. Zhuhai should fully leverage its advantages as a special economic zone and due to its location to accelerate the construction of transport infrastructures, build the transport hub on the west bank of the Pearl River Estuary as soon as possible, enhance the capability of the function of high-end factor agglomeration development and innovation development, the core competitiveness and its developmental driving ability, in order to become a modern central regional city, a new ecologically civilized special zone and a model city for scientific and technological development. This shows that there is an explicit functional positioning for Shenzhen and the Zhuhai Special Economic Zone in the Pearl River Delta Region of Guangdong Province in the new historical stage. However, since the State has clarified the important mission for Guangdong Province, especially for the Pearl River Delta Region, during the first implementation and experimentation, at the institutional system level, it will take time to turn all of the several special economic zones into free trade areas, an area where conditions permit or better development has been achieved. The Shenzhen Special Economic Zone should be chosen as a place where a free trade area can be built, which is undoubtedly an important choice for comprehensively pushing forward the regional economic integration in the new period. Therefore, the author believes that the direction of the future developmental path for China can be based on classified expansion, while expanding free trade areas or free ports should be the first choice for China's special economic zones in the future development of global special economic zones.

(II) **Basic conception of the building of free trade areas and free ports**

According to Paragraph (B) of Article 24 of the GATT, a free trade area means that customs duties and other restrictive trade laws and regulations are eliminated for, substantially, all trade in goods originating from a group of two or more customs territories between or among the territories of the members. In fact, in the practice of most of the established free trade areas in the world, the case where a free trade agreement involves more than 90% of the products in trade is deemed "substantially all the trade". According to relevant data, a free port mainly refers to the port where all or most of the foreign goods can enter and leave on a duty-free basis. Such a port is designated as being outside the customs territory of a country to the extent that foreign goods are duty-free when entering and leaving such a port and can be freely refitted, processed, stored for a long time, or sold. Only the goods which are transferred to consumers within the country where the free port is located are subject to customs duties; however, the inbound and outbound foreign ships must observe the laws, regulations and policies regarding health, immigration, etc.

1. **Shenzhen and Zhuhai towards free trade areas**

Both Shenzhen and Zhuhai are the special economic zones established the earliest after China's reform and opening up. With construction and development of more than 30 years, their city scale and level of development have preliminarily shown the embryonic form of a modern city, especially Shenzhen and Zhuhai which are adjacent to Hong Kong and Macau, respectively; therefore, based on consolidating the previous contacts and cooperation outcomes, with free trade development as a bond, the two kinds of special zones (special economic zones and special administrative regions) can further expand closer economic and trade relations to complement the functions, share the resources and improve each other, so as to promote a rapid development of the regional economy. As indicated by the relevant data, Shenzhen has achieved rapid economic development for many consecutive years, and especially the average annual economic growth rate has increased by more than 16% since 2002. Shenzhen's GDP hit 3306.7 billion yuan in 2008, up 9.0% compared with the previous year. The total value of goods imported and exported amounted to 2561.6 billion USD in Shenzhen in 2008, up 17.8%. The added value of new high-tech products accounted for 32.3% in Shenzhen in 2008. Zhuhai's GDP reached 99,206 million yuan in 2008, up 9%. Total imports and exports amounted to 39,869 million USD in Zhuhai in 2008, up 21.5%. Actually the exclusive used foreign direct investments reached 1142 million USD in Zhuhai in 2008, up 11.0%.[4] This fully demonstrates that the strength of Shenzhen and Zhuhai has certainly laid a foundation for building free trade areas.

2. **Xiamen and Shantou towards free ports**

Being opposite to the Taiwan Province of China, just across the Taiwan Straits, Xiamen and Shantou are seaport cities that have been given priority to developing during the new period in China. Historically, Xiamen was a world famous outward-looking port, while Shantou was also opened earlier and now is the important estuary for eastern Guangdong Province, southwestern Fujian Province, southern Jiangxi Province, and is at the southern end of the Beijing-Kowloon Railway. Shantou enjoys the important conditions for being developed into a free port. Xiamen and Shantou have witnessed a sustained economic and social development since their establishment as special zones. As a matter of fact, Xiamen's infrastructures, including railways, water transport, roads, and aviation, have been increasingly improved since China's reform and the opening up, earnestly promoting all-round economic and social development; it has given great contributions to the construction of the Western Taiwan Straits Economic Zone. With increasingly normal development of the relations across the Taiwan Straits, especially close economic and trade contacts and cooperation, the function of Xiamen's Port is becoming more and more important. Given such special status and roles, it is absolutely necessary and quite possible to build and develop Xiamen into

[4]Shenzhen, Zhuhai Bureau of Statistics, Shenzhen, Zhuhai Statistical Communiqués on National Economic and Social Development 2008.

a free port. This is also in accordance with the development of the world's economy and with the China's 11th Five-Year Developmental Plan. This will help the development of the Xiamen Special Economic Zone and the Western Taiwan Straits Economic Zone for the future sustainable development of Xiamen. The strategy needed to invigorate the city by relying on the port should be further implemented, and full play should be given to the new advantage of the Port of Xiamen in resource integration, stimulating Xiamen Free Port to play special important roles in construction of modernization in the new period. According to statistics, cargo throughput and container throughput in the Port of Shantou were 28.06 million tons and 0.72 million TEUs in 2008, up 22 and 21.1% compared with 2007, with a growth being 10.7 and 8.2% points higher than that in coastal ports above the designated size nationwide, respectively. Cargo throughput and container throughput at this port were 2.45 million tons and 58,000 TEUs in January, 2009, up 10.7 and 12%, respectively. In recent years, both the construction and the operation of the Port of Shantou have shown a great leap forward in growth. The Port of Shantou is designed to be built into a large, modern, multifunctional, integrated southeastern coastal 100-million-ton port opened to the outside world, laying an important foundation for the construction of the Shantou free port area.

3 The Necessity for Building the Shenzhen-Hong Kong-Zhuhai-Macau Free Trade Zone

(I) Free trade zones have become an important successful experience in enhancing regional units, leveraging the region's own advantages and better participating in international division and collaboration within regional global economic integration

According to relevant data, China will actively push forward with the construction of free trade zones, and further reinforce economic and trade cooperation with relevant countries and territories for promoting common development. China is reducing and eliminating customs duties and further opening up service and investment fields. China has achieved mutual benefits and win-win results with relevant countries and territories. For example, with the construction of the China-ASEAN Free Trade Area, more than 60% of the products have become duty-free in China and in the ASEAN area since 2008. Such a figure will most probably exceed 90% by 2010. According to relevant information, currently, China has conducted negotiations, provided business visas and joint study work concerning 14 free trade areas with 31 countries and territories. Seven free trade agreements have come into force and are well implemented. In order to better involve Guangdong Province, Hong Kong and Macau in regional global economic integration in the new period, it is imperative to further strengthen their integration and expand free trade areas with the regional characteristics of Shenzhen and Hong Kong. The practice in more than 30 years since China's reform and opening up has also fully proved that the Chinese Mainland, Hong Kong and Macau are highly complementary to each other in economic contacts and cooperation. A free trade area between Shenzhen and Zhuhai and the Hong Kong and Macau areas developed first in China, is also a new way of cooperation that is more suitable to boosting regional economic cooperation and integration after China's accession to the WTO. Such a new cooperation mode is conducive to strengthening economic and trade contacts under the principle of "One Country, Two Systems" and to advancing economic, trade cooperation and integration.

(II) CEPA has brought about tremendous achievements since its implementation in 2004; however, given the deep level, CEPA is still a necessary stage in the whole process of regional economic integration; as the special administrative regions of the People's Republic of China, Hong Kong and Macau need the Chinese Mainland to open up more fields so that Hong Kong and Macau can continuously increase a higher level of cooperation among the Chinese Mainland, Hong Kong and Macau

In fact, during the National People's Congress and the Chinese Political Consultative Conference in March, 2002, Hong Kong celebrities, including those from the Hong Kong General Chamber of Commerce, called for actively promoting the building of the Guangdong-Hong Kong-Macau Free Trade Area. The Hong Kong SAR Government also gave an impetus to its economic integration with the Chinese Mainland. Hong Kong's businessmen started vigorously moving ahead with the building of a free trade area between Hong Kong and the Chinese Mainland in the second half of that year. Hong Kong initiatively proposed to the Central Government with the hope of first initiating the free trade area in the Pearl River Delta Region.[5]

4 The Feasibility of Building the Shenzhen-Hong Kong-Zhuhai-Macau Free Trade Zone

(I) The Party and the State have vowed to implement the strategy for a free trade area in the new period, providing an explicit pointer for building the Shenzhen-Hong Kong-Zhuhai-Macau Free Trade Area

The Report of the 17th National Congress of the Communist Party of China stressed: "We shall actively carry out mutually beneficial international energy resource cooperation, implement the free trade area strategy, and strengthen bilateral and multilateral trade cooperation." This statement pinpoints the direction for setting up free trade areas with Chinese characteristics. Given the developmental pattern of the China-ASEAN Free Trade Area in which China would participate in

---

[5]Source: *Oriental News*, March 4, 2002.

2010, without doubt, this involves participation in the capacity of a country, while such a developmental pattern does not hinder the exploration regarding the developmental pattern of regional free trade areas within China, and building free trade areas with China's regional characteristics is one of the important choices.

(II) **In the new century, the State continues to expand the opening up and intensifying the reform; the plan for participating in world economic integration in the new period greatly promotes the attempt to build the new developmental model—the Shenzhen-Hong Kong-Zhuhai-Macau Free Trade Area with Chinese characteristics**

According to China's 11th Five-Year Plan for National Economic and Social Development, we must continuously intensify the reform and the opening up. We should insist on the socialist market economy as the reform direction, give overall considerations to both domestic development and the opening up, constantly increase the level of the opening up, and enhance the capability for boosting development under the condition of expanding the opening up. We should maintain the long-term prosperity and stability of Hong Kong and Macau. We should uphold the policy of "One Country, Two Systems", "Hong Kong people governing Hong Kong", "Macau people governing Macau", "high degree of autonomy", and act strictly in accordance with the basic law of the special administrative regions. We should reinforce and promote exchange and cooperation among the Chinese Mainland, Hong Kong and Macau in the fields of economics, trade, science, education, culture, health, and sports. We should continue carrying out closer economic partnership arrangements among the Chinese Mainland, Hong Kong and Macau. We should strengthen the cooperation among the Chinese Mainland, Hong Kong and Macau in the construction of infrastructures, inn industrial development, in the utilization of resources and in environmental protection. We should support Hong Kong in developing the service industry, including finance, logistics, tourism and information, and keep its position as the international financial, trade and shipping center. All of these will provide important conditions for attempting to build and develop the new developmental model—the Shenzhen-Hong Kong-Zhuhai-Macau Free Trade Area.

(III) **The timing for building the Shenzhen-Hong Kong-Zhuhai-Macau Free Trade Area**

As Hong Kong, Macau, Shenzhen and Zhuhai are subject to different political and social systems, the Shenzhen-Hong Kong-Zhuhai-Macau Free Trade Area will be built and developed under the "One Country, Two Systems" condition and according to the characteristic free trade area mode within the People's Republic of China. Given that Shenzhen and Zhuhai were the first to experiment in building a free trade area with Hong Kong and Macau, thus it was necessary to obtain the State's authorization and recognition. Therefore, the establishment of the Shenzhen-Hong Kong-Zhuhai-Macau Free Trade Area should be divided into two stages: first, Guangdong Province, Hong Kong and Macau hold consultations through high-level joint meetings to reach a consensus on jointly building the Shenzhen-Hong Kong-Zhuhai-Macau Free Trade Area, officially determine the geographic location for establishing the free trade area and its boundary line, specify other requirements for establishing the free trade area, apply to the Central Committee and the State Council for approval before the official launch. Second, the operating activities of the free trade area consistent with the actual developmental situation of Shenzhen, Hong Kong, Zhuhai and Macau are gradually carried out in stages mainly according to the WTO rules and the practices of free trade areas around the world.

5 Objective and Relevant Measures for Building the Shenzhen-Hong Kong-Zhuhai-Macau Free Trade Area

(I) The objective for building the Shenzhen-Hong Kong-Zhuhai-Macau Free Trade Area

The main and overall objective for building the Shenzhen-Hong Kong-Zhuhai-Macau Free Trade Area: based on the staged implementation of CEPA, it is necessary to further strengthen the economic and trade contacts among these four areas, comprehensively push forward their sustainable economic and trade development, carry out the operating activities completely, including economic and trade activities, within the whole area according to the requirements of free trade areas in line with the pattern of regional economic internationalization and integration and the actual situation of these special areas at different developmental stages as well as the rules concerning free trade areas. Besides, it is necessary to promote normal operations and coordinated development of the various economic and trade activities within the free trade area, conduct a scientific division of labor within the free trade area, rationally integrate various factors including commodities, goods, capital, talents and various services and complement their advantages within the free trade area to enhance the competitive power and international level of that area, and gradually liberalize goods, trade and investments in the free trade area.

(II) Relevant measures for building the Shenzhen-Hong Kong-Zhuhai-Macau Free Trade Area

1. First, cooperate with Hong Kong and Macau to follow international practices in order to uniformly define the standards, rules and specifications for trade in commodities, goods and services from Shenzhen and Zhuhai. Universally accepted rules in free trade areas require parties to adopt international standards, rules and specifications so as to effectively implement unified inspection procedures, making it possible to gradually achieve economic, trade and investment liberalization within the three areas.

2. Eliminate tariffs and all non-tariff restrictions on trade in commodities and goods. As Hong Kong and Macau are free ports, as members of the free trade area, Shenzhen and Zhuhai should, like Hong Kong and Macau, eliminate, in stages, tariffs and other relevant non-tariff restrictions relating to various commodities and goods according to the unified principles or practices which satisfy the operating requirements for the free trade area in transactions involving commodities or goods, trade and services. The current tariffs concerning commodities or goods and trade among the members should be eliminated according to percentages in the transition period of 3–5 years through consultation by the parties. The 1st stage: the first reduction would be made within one year after the agreement regarding the Shenzhen-Hong Kong-Zhuhai-Macau Free Trade Area comes into force. In this case, the members of the free trade area would reduce and exempt or eliminate 20% according to the uniformly verified current tariff base for relevant products. The 2nd stage: a further 30% reduction, exemption or elimination on the basis of the 1st stage within three years after the agreement of the Shenzhen-Hong Kong-Zhuhai-Macau Free Trade Area comes into force. All of the remaining 50% would be eliminated within five years after the agreement comes into force. In addition, the members of the free trade area should eliminate, in stages, all non-tariff restrictions as from the date when the signed agreement comes into force and undertake not to impose any new restrictive measures again. This enables a fully and highly free operation of all commodities and goods within the free trade area and full alignment with the operating activities of free trade areas around the world.
3. Take measures to earnestly push forward and promote trade and investment facilitations among the members of the Shenzhen-Hong Kong-Zhuhai-Macau Free Trade Area. The free trade area is a developmental model at a higher level on the basis of preferential trade arrangements (CEPA), thus undoubtedly, trade and investment facilitations among the members of the free trade area should be the operating activities for implementing further free and higher trade and investment facilitation measures, so as to provide the members of the free trade area with more convenient, easier, efficient functions regarding their operating activities, and promote the healthy development of economic, trade and investment integration within the free trade area. Of course, relevant policies should also be adopted to simplify the procedures for exchanges, communications and interactions in the circles of industrial and commercial enterprises among the members of the free trade area, to the greatest extent reduce the barriers prohibiting the movement of people within the free trade area, simplify trade settlement procedures, periodically or non-periodically hold economic and trade fairs and exhibitions, carry out other economic and trade activities.
4. Develop a system for the protection of investments in order to secure an interest win-win outcome among the members within the free trade area. The implementation of China's reform and opening-up policy has promoted the overall economic and social development of Shenzhen, Hong Kong, Zhuhai and Macau. After the Shenzhen-Hong Kong-Zhuhai-Macau Free Trade Area is established, the requirements of the WTO rules for encouraging and protecting mutual investments should be earnestly put into practice, and an investment protection system

complying with WTO rules and free trade area requirements should be developed and improved through consultations on the basis of continuously improving the investment environment and following the principle of reciprocity, mutual benefit and win-win outcome, with a view to fundamentally raising the enthusiasm for mutual investment among the members of the free trade area and thus enhancing the foundation and global competitive power of the free trade area.

Reference

1. Zhong Jian (2006) A Study of Developmental Models for Special Economic Zones around the World, China Economic Publishing House

A New Stage of China's Economy and the New Practice of Binhai New Area Development and Opening Up

Gang Liu

Abstract China's economic and social development has entered a new developmental stage. The traditional economic developmental model, driven by comparative advantages and "factor rent", has laid bare a series of problems and drawbacks while bringing about the rapid growth and development of China's economy for 30 years. Sustained economic and social development requires new driving forces during the new developmental stage. How to seek out a new developmental model driven by competitive advantages and "innovation rent" in the new round of reform and opening up is an issue which must be addressed first during the new stage. After 2005, the national comprehensive reform pilot areas represented by Shanghai's Pudong, the Binhai New Area of Tianjin and the Shenzhen Special Zone were launched, which was the preliminary attempt made by the State to explore a new developmental model. Since the development and the opening up of the Binhai New Area of Tianjin was incorporated into the national overall developmental strategy, with a focus on building a research and development transformation base, many new beneficial practices have been carried out in exploring a new developmental model, and the resulting new experience is of positive inspirational significance for China's economic development.

Keywords New stage of the economy · Factor rent · Innovation rent

30 years ago—at the end of 1978, China seized the historical opportunity offered by economic globalization to achieve sustained and rapid economic and social development in China by carrying out market-oriented reforms of the economic system and the opening up policy. With the 30-year-long rapid economic growth and development, China has entered a new developed stage amid new changes in the domestic and international environment in the 21st century. The disadvantages

Liu Gang (1965—), Deputy Director, Professor, Nankai Institute of Economics

G. Liu (✉)
Binhai Development Research Institute, Nankai University, 300071 Tianjin, China

Y. Yuan (ed.), *Studies on China's Special Economic Zones*, Research Series on the Chinese Dream and China's Development Path,
DOI 10.1007/978-981-10-3704-7_10

and drawbacks of the traditional economic developmental model have surfaced since 2005, especially under the impact of the global financial crisis. Economic development calls for new driving forces under the new historical conditions; the new driving forces come from the new institutional changes and more open integration into the international economy and community. How to find a new model of economic development by intensifying the reform of the socialist market economy system under the guidance of the outlook on scientific development is the first issue for China during the new developmental stage. The Binhai New Area of Tianjin has accumulated the wisdom and experience from home and abroad to actively explore a new economic developmental model since 2005, while the resulting new approaches and new practices will offer experience and reference for us.

1 Two Kinds of Strategic Thoughts and Developmental Models Regarding China's Economy Since the Reform and the Opening Up

(I) Two kinds of strategic ways of thinking regarding China's economy since the reform and the opening up

Tremendous achievements have been made in China's economy since the reform and the opening up which started at the end of 1978. According to statistics, China's GDP, the total import and export trade, fiscal revenue in 2007 were 67.7, 105.3 and 45.3 times what they were in 1978, respectively.[1] With the rapid economic growth, China's economic structures, social structures, institutional structures and international economic relations have changed profoundly. The rapid growth of China's economy has become the main source for world economy and trade. More importantly, China still enjoys a huge potential for economic growth and may become the country with the fastest economic growth and development in the 21st century.

Thirty years of economic and social development in China is a process of making progressive changes in the economic and social system to gradually move towards an open socialist market economy and explore a socialist economic developmental path with Chinese characteristics. Such a developmental process has always been accompanied by two different ways of thinking or modes of economic development. First, emphasizing the theory of comparative advantage which is part of orthodox economics, attempting to rely on "factor rent" to stimulate rapid economic growth; second, stressing the division of labor based on specialization and disruptive innovation, attempting to rely on "innovation rent" and competitive advantage to achieve a great leap forward in economic development. In reality, the

[1]National Bureau of Statistics of the People's Republic of China, Statistical Communiqué on National Economic and Social Development, China Statistical Yearbook (1979–2008), China Statistics Press.

Latin American mode and the Japanese-South Korean mode and their experience, separately, correspond to both kinds of strategic ways of thinking or modes. With regard to open market-oriented institutional change, as both kinds of strategic thinking or modes involve different understandings of the driving forces for economic growth and development, the former emphasizes simple deregulation and optimization of the investment environment, while the latter stresses the building of an entrepreneurial or innovation environment.

(II) The impact of two kinds of strategic thinking on the course of economic development

At different developmental stages, both kinds of developmental ways of thinking or modes have always affected the actual process of China's economic development. However, depending upon the historical conditions at the specific stage of economic development, a way of thinking or mode may have the dominant position at a certain stage, thus China's economic growth and development has taken a certain path and track.

1. The traditional mode of economic growth driven by "factor rent"

There was an excessive emphasis on relying on comparative advantages to promote China's economic growth and development before 2005, thus forming a model of economic development that was driven by "factor rent" in line with specific historical conditions.

The traditional model of economic development was based on comparative advantages, under which comparative advantages, especially factor resource advantages such as cheap labor, land and environment, were considered as China's resource endowment; so simple deregulation was conducted and the investment environment was optimized to initiate private investments and attract FDI for using cheap resources to obtain factor rent.[2] Under the traditional developmental model, on the one hand, foreign capital was introduced to rapidly integrate China's economy into the world economy and extensive international economic circulation, and make China an important manufacturing base in the world; on the other hand, the economic management functions of the government were transformed, state-owned enterprises were reformed and private investments were initiated to gradually develop a market-based resource allocation mechanism.

However, whether private investments were initiated or foreign capital was introduced, the traditional economic developmental model emphasized the utilization and allocation of cheap labor, land and other resources. Such a model of economic development with high dependence on resources and capital input generated great

[2]This can be seen from the design of the objective for attracting foreign capital at the beginning of China's reform and opening up. As the competitive power of China's manufacturing industry was low at the beginning of reform and the opening up, the main objective of the export-oriented policy for attracting foreign capital at that time was to earn foreign exchange, followed by increasing employment and taxes.

achievements in economic development, but resulted in a heavy price—excessive development of resources and environmental pollution which occurred at the early stage of development in developed countries. In terms of the mode of economic growth, currently China is beset by various acute problems including high input, high consumption, high emission, lack of coordination, difficulty in circulation and low efficiency, and severe hidden problems regarding development.[3]

According to statistical data, China's traditional model of economic development was driven by factor input. China's incremental capital-output ratio increased from 1:1.8 during the years 1981–1985 to 1:4.99 during the years 2001–2004. The extensive factor input-driven mode led to a faster consumption of resources in China while spurring a rapid growth of China's economy. China's GDP was 2.64 trillion USD based on the prevailing exchange rate in 2006, accounting for about 5.46% of the world's GDP; however, the consumed resources, including crude oil, raw coal, iron ore, steel, aluminum oxide and cement, made up about 7.4, 31, 30, 27, 25 and 40% of the world's consumption, respectively, and the resource consumption was much higher than the world's average level.[4] High input and high consumption drove rapid economic growth, but also gave rise to high emissions and heavy pollution; the wastewater discharge resulting from increasing a unit of GDP in China was 4 times higher than that in developed countries; the solid wastes generated by a unit of industrial output value in China were 10 times more than those in developed countries (see Footnote 4).

The traditional model of economic development under which a high economic growth was achieved by high input and high consumption of resources and factors has led to uncoordinated structural development of China's economy. First, compared with the rapid development of the industry, China's agricultural foundation is still weak, and the issues concerning agriculture, rural areas and farmers have existed for a long time; second, the development of the modern service industry is slow compared with the development of the manufacturing industry. Currently, the added value of China's service industry accounts for only 32.3% of the GDP, lower than both the world's average level (66.4%) and the average level of low-income countries (45%) (see Footnote 4); third, China is only at the low end of the global industrial value chain and the external sources of technologies have severely restricted the improvement in the international competitive power of China's manufacturing industry; finally, the gap in residents' income distribution has become increasingly wide amid the high economic growth. The Gini coefficient which reflects China's residents' income gap has been generally on the increase since the reform and the opening up. According to the statistics from the World

---

[3]Xu Youlong, Ma Kai Discusses Scientific Development, *Observation & Thinking*, 2004(15), quoted from Xu Youlong, What Growth Mode is Needed for China? *Observation & Thinking*, 2004(15).

[4]Xu Youlong, What Growth Mode is Needed for China? *Observation & Thinking*, 2004(15).

Bank, China's Gini coefficient was 0.16 before the reform and the opening up and reached 0.458 in 2003, exceeding the internationally-accepted alarm level (0.4), thus being on the verge of danger.[5]

2. **Four basic characteristics of the traditional model of economic development**

Given the actual reality of China's economic development, the traditional model of economic development merely based on comparative advantages is unsustainable. Subject to rising factor costs and a deteriorating foreign trade environment, a host of labor-intensive enterprises in the Pearl River Delta, where the manufacturing clusters first flourished thanks to China's reform and opening up, have gone bankrupt and have relocated to other areas since 2007.[6] China's economic situation has become grim due to the global financial crisis, thus we have to reflect on the disadvantages and drawbacks of the traditional model of economic development.

Reviewing the 30-year course of China's rapid economic growth and development, we can conclude that the tremendous achievements made are mainly attributable to the fact that the market-oriented reform and opening-up policy gave scope to and amplified the comparative advantages based on resource factor endowments. However, the economic developmental way of thinking and mode based on the comparative advantages of resources and factors have caused many hidden problems in development while delivering high growth to China's economy. Transforming the economic developmental way of thinking and mode is the fundamental way to eliminate these hidden problems.

This paper summarizes the basic characteristics of China's traditional economic developmental way of thinking or mode in the following four aspects: (1) underscoring the roles of comparative advantages and "factor rent" in driving the economic growth, with comparative advantages mainly including cheap labor, land and other resource advantages; (2) laying stress on the introduction of technologies and production manufacturing, overlooking self-independent innovation, research and development, pursuing an extensive expansion of the economic scale, ignoring the intensive growth of the economy; (3) Practicing an extensive mode of economic growth, excessively relying on input and resource consumption, stressing the role of both investment and foreign capital as driving forces for economic growth;

[5]Quoted from China's Gini Coefficient Approaching 0.47, Seven Measures for Narrowing the Income Gap, March 13, 2006, http://www.xinhuanet.com.

[6]See the report "Survey on Closedown of about 1000 Enterprises in the Pearl River Delta: Rising Costs Caused Enterprises to Relocate to Other Areas" by CCTV *Half-Hour Economy* (December 10, 2007). As reported by the *Southern Metropolis Daily* on January 22, 2008, in January of the new year, the Pearl River Delta was undergoing unprecedented pain of transfer: about 1000 shoe factories were closed down, and more than 10,000 Hong Kong-funded enterprises were facing a wave of closure, a large number of small and medium-sized enterprises were planning to relocate. In early March, 2008, the *Wall Street Journal* reported that nearly 10,000 foreign-funded enterprises in the Pearl River Delta were closed down or had been moved to other areas.

(4) being government-led and thus overemphasizing the economic growth rate, with the government policy system focusing on deregulation of private investments and the optimization of the investment environment for foreign capital.

2 The New Stage of China's Economic and Social Development and a New Round of Economic Transformation

(I) New characteristics of economic development determine the necessity to transform strategic ways of thinking

The disadvantages of the traditional model of economic development have been gradually exposed since 2005. With new changes in the domestic and international environment, China's economy is entering a new stage of development.

China's economic development shows a series of new-stage characteristics during the new stage of economic development. National economic strength has significantly improved, while the overall level of the productive forces and the capability for independent innovation are not high, and long-standing structural contradictions and an extensive growth mode have not been fundamentally changed yet. The socialist market economy system has preliminarily taken shape, but the obstacles due to institutions and to the mechanism affecting the economic development still exist, and further reform in difficult areas meets with deep-seated contradictions and problems. People's lives have generally reached the affluent level, but the tendency towards the widening of the income distribution gap has not yet been fundamentally reversed, and the urban and rural poverty-stricken population and low-income population are still at a considerable size; prominent achievements have been made in coordinated development, while the situation in which the agricultural foundation remains weak and the rural development still lags behind has not changed yet, and the task for narrowing the rural, urban and regional gap in development and promoting coordinated economic and social development is arduous. The opening up is expanding, international competition is becoming increasingly fierce, and the pressure from the dominance which the developed countries enjoy in the economy, science and technology will continue to exist for a long time. More and more risks which can be and are hardly predictable are cropping up. The requirements for giving overall considerations to domestic development and the opening up are becoming higher.[7]

In view of these characteristics of China's economic development during the new stage, it is essential to transform the strategic way of thinking and mode of economic development, while carrying out an outlook on scientific development is

[7]Hu Jintao, "Hold High the Great Banner of Socialism with Chinese Characteristic and Strive for New Victories in Building a Moderately Prosperous Society in all Respects—Report in the 17th National Congress of the Communist Party of China", October 15, 2007.

the core and key to exploring a new model of development (see Footnote 7). According to the requirements of the outlook on scientific development, the driving forces for economic growth and development are no longer "factor rent" based on resource endowment; instead, these driving forces are "innovation rent" based on knowledge and technical innovations. At the level of institutional change, building the institutional environment which centers on self-independent innovation and effectively promotes entrepreneurship and innovations is the important way for realizing an outlook on scientific development. In essence, the exploration of a new model of economic development is the second economic transformation in China and is a process of forming and developing a self-independent innovation path with Chinese characteristics and an innovative economy.

(II) The new way of thinking of economic development must realize transformation regarding five aspects

Given the actual situation of China's economic development, compared with the traditional model of economic development, the new economic developmental mode of thinking must bring about transformation regarding the following five aspects:

First, transformation from the extensive growth mode to the intensive growth mode. In order to transform to the intensive growth mode, it is necessary to change the practice of simply pursuing scale expansion, emphasize the technical renovation of enterprises, self-independent innovations and efforts to tap the enterprises' potential in internal management; furthermore, it is essential to increase the science and technology input of the enterprises so as to upgrade their products and services, enhance the international competitive advantages of the enterprises. Actions should be taken to innovate in the traditional mode of production organization and to explore an organizational mode which suits China's national conditions and enables sustainable innovations and flexible manufacturing within the enterprises. Efforts should focus on using IT to propel industrialization, promoting IT development through industrialization, undertaking a new road towards industrialization.

Second, transformation from a resource-consuming mode to a resource-saving, environmentally-friendly one. During economic development, it is necessary to save and comprehensively utilize resources, vigorously develop a recycling economy, and explore the model of economic development based on recycling: "resources-products-renewable resources". The State should strengthen the strict management of resources and intensify ecological environmental protection.

Third, transformation from technology introduction to technical innovations. The knowledge necessary for innovations is basically implicit knowledge and is strictly restricted by spatial scope. At the current stage of China's manufacturing development, the enhancement of its international competitive advantages mainly relies on the implicit knowledge which cannot be achieved by direct introduction from foreign countries, simple learning and imitation; such enhancement is a result of long-term knowledge accumulation.

Fourth, transformation from a foreign capital-driven mode to a domestic demand-led one. China has basically taken an outward-looking road towards economic development after 30 years of reform and the opening up; however, the international environment is complicated and changing, posing severe security problems to China's economic development and bringing no benefits to increasing the national welfare level.

Fifth, transformation from capital import to capital export. Chinese enterprises have found it difficult to carry out transnational operations since the beginning of the 21st century; the root cause is that these enterprises have based their competitive advantages on the comparative advantages of domestic resources and factors. As Chinese enterprises have improved in self-independent innovations and their technological level, transnational operations are an inevitable choice for them. The issue concerning how to help and guide Chinese enterprises to perform transnational operations must be addressed during the new stage of economic development.

Being different from the traditional model of economic development, the new model of economic development has the following characteristics: (1) emphasizing the roles of competitive advantages and "innovation rent" in stimulating economic growth and development, with competitive advantages based on the innovations of new knowledge and its commercialization; (2) laying stress on self-independent innovation, research and development of technologies, pursuing to speed up the economy and its intensive growth; (3) practicing the intensive mode of economic growth, relying on the creation and commercialization of new knowledge; (4) adopting a system of government policies focusing on building an entrepreneurial and innovative environment rather than deregulating private investments and optimizing the investment environment for foreign capital.

3 Exploration of the New Model of Development in the Binhai New Area of Tianjin

(I) Developmental positioning of the Binhai New Area of Tianjin

According to the Opinions of the State Council on Issues Concerning Promoting the Development and Opening-up of the Binhai New Area and the Overall Plan for Comprehensive Reform Experiment in the Binhai New Area of Tianjin, the developmental goal for the Binhai New Area of Tianjin is specified as follows: in 5–10 years, first develop a well-improved system of a socialist market economy in the Binhai New Area, continuously enhance the area's capability for innovation and service and the international competitiveness of the Binhai New Area, play a bigger role in driving the development of Tianjin, push forward the economic revival in Beijing, Tianjin, Hebei Province and in the Circum-Bohai-sea Region, promote the interaction among the eastern, central and western regions and the national coordinated economic development, offer experience and a model for national development and reforms.

Given the domestic and international conditions during the new stage of China's economic development, the trends of the economic development in the Circum-Bohai-sea Region and the actual local situation, the Binhai New Area of Tianjin will become a world-class city. It is based on the manufacturing industry with a high capability for self-independent innovation, and it has the comprehensive functions of an international financial, trade, shipping and logistics center; it can play an active role in China's involvement in global economic activities as well as having an international economic influence. The Binhai New Area will serve as a platform for economic dialogue between China and the world, a gateway for the opening up and an engine for stimulating the economic development of Northern China.

As a world-class city, the Binhai New Area must be developed by relying on its own innovation capability, developmental vitality, service capability and international competitiveness to integrate domestic and international resources so as to foster common regional economic and social development and prosperity. In order to advance the development and the opening-up of the Binhai New Area, the State gives the Binhai New Area the priority right to first implementation and experimentation in comprehensive supplementary reforms and institutional space for innovation rather than simple preferential policies. Therefore, being different from the traditional development and opening-up mode, the development and opening-up of the Binhai New Area depends on the innovative advantages and "innovation rent" generated by a series of institutional innovations instead of preferential policies and "factor rent". Thus, the new developmental model of the Binhai New Area has a special connotation, route and mechanism—improving the socialist market mechanism and intensifying the reform and opening up, relying on the institutional space for innovation to spur self-independent innovation so as to obtain innovation advantages and "innovation rent", sharpen the international competitive edge of enterprises, industries and the region. First it is necessary to transform from a manufacturing economy to an innovative economy, achieve, scientific and harmonious development first.

(II) Exploration of the new developmental model in the Binhai New Area and the framework of its mode

Since the development and the opening-up of the Binhai New Area was incorporated into the overall national strategy for development, the new developmental model has been explored mainly regarding the following three aspects: first, making institutional innovations to improve the system of a socialist market economy; second, utilizing the institutional innovation advantages to make full use of new opportunities available at home and abroad so as to form and develop the functions of a modern transformation base for manufacturing, research and development, an international financial, trade, shipping and logistics center; third, carrying out the construction of infrastructures and ecological environment which matches with the above contents.

According to the Overall Plan for a Comprehensive Reform Experiment in the Binhai New Area of Tianjin, as shown by the embryonic form of the Binhai New Area of Tianjin which is being explored and developed, the framework of the new mode mainly covers the following aspects:

1. **Build a more perfect system of a socialist market economy capable of effectively supporting self-independent innovation**

Given the deep-seated institutional obstacles in reform, the following two aspects will be highlighted to intensify the reform of the economic system and improve the system of the socialist market economy in the Binhai New Area of Tianjin:

First, intensify the reform of enterprises, develop a mixed ownership economy, establish and improve the micro foundation for the socialist market economy basically by centering on developing the modern manufacturing industry and the modern service industry, giving prominence to strategic adjustments of the state-owned economy in order to intensify the reform of the system of property rights of the state-owned enterprises, accelerating the establishment of a modern enterprise system, innovating the model of enterprise development, optimizing the enterprise developmental environment, enhancing the vitality and competitiveness of the enterprises.

Invigorate large enterprises while relaxing the control over the small ones to further reform the system of property rights at the state-owned enterprises, establish a modern enterprise system and cultivate the self-reliance ability of enterprises. Vigorously develop and support the non-public sectors of the economy, to enter such fields as financial service, public utility and infrastructures. Optimize the institutional environment for the entrepreneurship, growth and development of enterprises, tirelessly enhance the innovation capability and the international competitiveness of enterprises. Encourage the development of small and medium-sized innovative enterprises, and build an integrated public service platform for small and medium-sized enterprises.

With a view to encouraging the development of small and medium-sized innovative enterprises, 6 national-level new and high technology bases for industrialization, more than 40 enterprise incubators are being built and a number of self-owned brands at an advanced domestic level are being cultivated in Tianjin and the Binhai New Area. Many projects which are being incubated have shown obvious self-independent innovation advantages.

Second, deepen the reform of the scientific and technological system, develop a regional innovation system, enhance the self-independent innovation capability of enterprises, and build high-level transformation bases for research and development. Focus on speeding up the commercialization of research findings and technologies, improve a market-oriented enterprise-focused institutional framework for self-independent innovation, enhance the overall innovation capability, and by 2010, turn the Binhai New Area of Tianjin into the forerunner of an innovation-oriented city.

The overall objective for self-independent innovation in the Binhai New Area of Tianjin is to build an innovation-oriented new area where the layout of the park and the division of labor are clear, a centralized construction of science and technology project is conducted, and innovation resources are effectively allocated, and where the industry, universities and research institutions are closely integrated. First, promote the transformation of scientific and technological achievements into productive forces, establish the Binhai Venture Capital Investment Guidance Fund worth 2 billion yuan and introduce foreign venture capital organizations; second, create an environment beneficial to innovation, earnestly introduce and cultivate various outstanding talents and innovation teams; third, give scope to the role of enterprises as the main body in innovation, attract multinational corporations and leading domestic enterprises to set up research and development institutions, engineering centers and form high technology industrial clusters. Give priority to pushing ahead with the construction of 12 scientific and technological platforms including a national-level international biopharmaceutical innovation park, an industrial biotechnology research and development center, a civil aviation science and technology industrial base, and build 10 industrial technology research and development centers involving steel pipes, textiles and automobiles.

2. **Establish factor market systems including modern financial service systems**

First, push forward financial reform innovation, set up a modern financial service system suitable for a socialist market economy system. Subject to ensuring that risks are controllable, act in a scientific and prudent way to focus on expanding direct financing and enhancing the comprehensive service function of financial enterprises, actively press ahead with comprehensive financial reforms, build a modern financial service system fit for the development and the opening-up of the North Economic Center and the Binhai New Area, develop the national financial reform innovation base, and establish a more vibrant, more open financial system.

Broaden direct financing channels, improve the social capital structure, increase the efficiency of social capital utilization, and gradually develop Tianjin into China's center for the issuance of industrial investment funds, management, trading, information and talent training. Carry out a pilot comprehensive operation of financial enterprises, and enhance the service function of financial enterprises. Introduce domestic and international financial institutions, gradually develop them into the North Financial Center. Reform the foreign exchange management system, establish a trading market for national non-listed public company equities, and optimize the financial environment.

Second, quicken the construction of a modern market system. Build Tianjin into the North International Trade Center by speeding up the construction of large commodity trading markets covering petrochemical engineering, coal, steel, cotton and grain, and exploring the trading business of commodity forward contracts.

Third, follow the principle of unified planning, law-based management, market allocation and government regulations to optimize the structure of land use, innovate the inland management mode so as to shape a new pattern of land saving and intensive land use in which the cultivated land resources are really protected and attention is given to the efficiency of land assets.

3. **Intensify the reform of foreign-related systems, give full play to Tianjin's role as the gateway to the opening up, gradually turn Tianjin into the international trade and shipping center of Northern China**

With a focus on building the Dongjiang Bonded Port Area, accelerate the construction of the North International Shipping Center and International Logistics Center. Make reference to internationally accepted practices, mainly develop international transshipment, international distribution, international procurement, international entrepôt trade and exporting processing in the Dongjiang Bonded Port Area, and where conditions permit, make reform exploration to build a free trade port.

Intensify the institutional reforms concerning foreign capital, promote the effective utilization of foreign capital and diversification of utilization modes. Actively implement the "go global" strategy, build a service platform for enterprises to "go global", encourage and standardize enterprises' investment cooperation in foreign countries, and develop those enterprises which satisfy the conditions into multinational corporations.

Innovate the cooperation mode in the East Asian Region, establish a closer economic and trade cooperation mechanism among the Binhai New Area of Tianjin, North China and the areas which enjoy special opening-up policies in Northeast Asian countries, such as Japan and South Korea, in order to intensify and enhance Northeast Asian regional cooperation.

4. **Push forward the reform of system of urban and rural planning management, promote a harmonious development of the Binhai New Area and urban areas, build new ecological urban areas**

Focus on implementing the overall urban plan for Tianjin and the overall urban plan for the Binhai New Area, reform the system of urban and rural planning management, strengthen the supervision and management of plan implementation, reinforce the protection of ecological environmental resources, build new ecological urban areas, a harmonious development of people and nature, an economic, social and ecological environment.

Center on intensifying a comprehensive rural reform and break through the institutional obstacles resulting in urban-rural segmentation, balance the urban and rural development, promote urban and rural integration in the management system, policy support, industrial distribution and public service, accelerate urbanization, build a demonstration area for the development of urban and rural integration.

5. **Push forward reforms in social and public management fields, innovate the public service management system, build a basic public service system covering urban and rural areas**

Reform the systems involving resource conservation and environmental protection, develop a recycling economy, build a conservation-minded, environmentally-friendly society. Innovate the public service governance mechanism and supervision system, place more emphasis on social equity, address the issues concerning the most immediate, realistic interests which people are most concerned with, increase the supply of public services, speed up the construction of a basic public service system which can meet the needs of domestic and foreign personnel, provide rational, moderate social security and cover both urban and rural areas.

With environmental optimization and economic growth as the core, in order to build new ecological urban areas, center on saving energy, water, materials, land and comprehensive utilization of resources, earnestly develop a recycling economy, propel the optimization and upgrading of economic distribution, industrial and product structure, turn the Binhai New Area into a national demonstration area for building a resource-saving, environmentally-friendly society.

4 Summative Review

As indicated by the experimentation on the new model of economic development in the Binhai New Area of Tianjin since 2005, the key points of the new mode driven by "innovation rent" are creation, commercialization and application of new knowledge, changes and innovations in the corresponding economic and social systems. The new model of economic development is guided by an outlook on scientific development. The core question answered by this new mode involves how to undertake a self-independent innovation path with Chinese characteristics or shape China's innovative economy. Essentially, it is the second transformation of China's economy.

In the new round of development and opening-up of the Binhai New Area, institutional changes and opening-up policies center on stimulating self-independent innovations within Chinese enterprises and industries, while institutional innovation focuses on the building of an entrepreneurial or innovation environment rather than a simple deregulation and optimization of the investment environment. With a focus on transformation from a production-oriented manufacturing economy to a research and development-driven innovative economy, the Binhai New Area has witnessed a deepening understanding of the socialist market economy system. Building a modern financial service system, a scientific and technological system, a public service and management system commensurate with the entrepreneurial or innovative economy is the top priority in the establishment of the socialist market economy system. The market system necessary for the entrepreneurial or innovative economy is not closed but it is more open. Intensifying the experimentation on the new developmental model, people in the Binhai New Area of Tianjin have gradually realized that under new domestic and international conditions, only when we first initiate and develop the innovative economy in the development and opening-up of the Binhai New Area and transform the Binhai New Area from a manufacturing economy to an innovative economy, can the new mode in the Binhai New Area be of real model significance for national economic and social development.

A Study of the Unique Characteristics of the Development and Opening-Up of the Pudong New Area of Shanghai

Li Youlin

Abstract The development of the Pudong New Area of Shanghai was initiated in response to a pressing situation. The background of such a situation exactly endowed Pudong with a different connotation of the times and unique characteristics. In a short period of 18 years since Pudong's development and opening up, an outward-looking, multifunctional modern new urban area rose on the east bank of the Pudong. It is hailed as the symbol of China's reform and opening up and the epitome of Shanghai's construction modernization. The key to the unique characteristics of the Pudong New Area's development and opening up lies in innovation. The "new" unique characteristics of the Pudong New Area can be explained by the following five aspects: the role mission of the national strategy, factor characteristics of a market economy, the evolution of governmental functions, integration and harmony of social development, building of an innovation-driven development of a first-class Party.

Keywords Pudong development · Connotation of the times · Unique characteristics

1 Introduction

Researching the unique characteristics of Pudong's development and opening up is of great practical significance for reviewing and summarizing the great undertaking of China's reform and opening up, analyzing and interpreting the strategic pattern of China's reform and opening up, spurring a new round of comprehensive reform. The key of the unique characteristics of Pudong's development and opening up lies in innovation. The "newness" of the Pudong New Area is embodied in not only building an outward-looking, multifunctional modern "new" city, but also exploring a "new" path for first establishing and improving the socialist market economy system under the guidance of the socialist theory with Chinese characteristics. As a

---

L. Youlin (✉)
Publicity Department of the Pudong New Area, Shanghai 200135, China

Y. Yuan (ed.), *Studies on China's Special Economic Zones*, Research Series on the Chinese Dream and China's Development Path,
DOI 10.1007/978-981-10-3704-7_11

successful practice of the socialist road with Chinese characteristics, Pudong's development and opening up was designed to fulfill the historical mission of a national strategy, functioning as a flagship, serving as a window. It has brought about breakthroughs in the developmental model of a market economy, factor agglomeration, the characteristics of the opening-up, explorations in streamlining governmental administration, first developing a plan, fostering a business-friendly environment for business promotion, and innovations in urban and rural integration for social development, co-construction and sharing, a humanistic spirit. It has also guaranteed the building of a first-class Party for promoting first-rate development, and has stressed that an uncorrupt government also represents an investment environment.

With regard to China's 30-year-long reform and opening up, its form mainly changed from special zones to new areas, from new areas to comprehensive reform pilot areas, including 53 national-level high and new technology developmental zones, 15 bonded areas, 57 export processing zones; geographically, it mainly advanced along the following four lines: three north-south lines from the five special zones in Southern China to Pudong of Shanghai and Binhai of Tianjin for the revitalization of northeastern China (extensive opening up in the eastern coastal areas), from Beijing, Wuhan, Changsha-Zhuzhou-Xiangtan to Shenzhen (the rise of Central China), from Chongqing to Chengdu and the Beibu Gulf (development of the western regions), and one east-west line from Pudong of Shanghai to Wuhan of the Hubei Province, from Changsha-Zhuzhou-Xiangtan of the Hunan Province to Chengdu of Sichuan and Chongqing. The three north-south lines existed for exactly 30 years, while the three north-south lines and one east-west line constitute the shape of the Chinese character 卅 which means 30. Such a coincidence agrees with the strategic map of China's reform and opening up. This strategic layout has two important nodes: Shenzhen of Guangdong and Pudong of Shanghai. The concept, as described in the academic circles, from "five specials and one newness" (five special economic zones including Shenzhen, Zhuhai, Shantou, Xiamen and Hainan, and the Pudong New Area) to "five newnesses and one special" (Pudong, Binhai, Wuhan, Changsha-Zhuzhou-Xiangtan, Chengdu-Chongqing in a new round of reform experimentation approved by the State, and Shenzhen as a "comprehensive reform area beyond a comprehensive reform area") also reflects the important position of Shenzhen and Pudong in the pattern of China's reform and opening up. Such a position also determines the intrinsic unique characteristics of Pudong's development and opening up.

The key to the unique characteristics of Pudong's development and opening up is "newness". The "newness" of the Pudong New Area is embodied in not only building an outward-looking, multifunctional modern "new" city, but also in exploring a "new" path for first establishing and improving a socialist market economy system under the guidance of the socialist theory with Chinese characteristics. The Central Committee of the Communist Party of China and the State Council announced the development and opening-up of Pudong of Shanghai on April 18, 1990, elevating Pudong's development from a local concept to a national strategy. The Executive Meeting of the State Council approved Pudong to be the first to launch a pilot comprehensive reform on June 21, 2005, foregrounding Pudong in the wave of reform again. In a short period of 18 years since Pudong's development and opening up, an outward-looking, multifunctional modern new urban area rose on the east bank of Pudong, which was hailed as the symbol of China's reform and opening up and the epitome of Shanghai's construction modernization.[1] The "new" characteristics of Pudong can be analyzed from the following five perspectives.

2 The Role Mission of the National Strategy

Unlike the four special economic zones established in China in 1980 and the Hainan Special Economic Zone set up in 1988, Pudong's development and opening-up was a major strategic decision made by the Central Committee of the Communist Party of China and Comrade Deng Xiaoping by proceeding from the overall situation of China's reform and opening up and construction modernization against the new special historical background.

(I) Political mission

After the political disturbance in the late spring and early summer of 1989, some people at home and abroad assumed a skeptical attitude toward whether to continue the path for reform and opening up or not; economic development slowed down for several consecutive years. Based on clear judgment about such an overall situation, when talking with leading members of the Central Committee of the Communist Party of China in 1989, Comrade Deng Xiaoping pointed out: "Now the international community is worrying that we will tighten the policy of reform and opening up, thus we must do several things to show that our policy of reform and opening up is unchanged and we will further advance reform and the opening up." He added: "I have retired, but we want to emphasize one thing: The development of Pudong of Shanghai; you need to pay more attention to this. Shanghai enjoys obvious advantages in talents, technologies and management. Shanghai is our trump card."[2] Comrade Deng Xiaoping once said: "If Pudong had developed a few years earlier, like the Shenzhen Special Economic Zone, Pudong's development would exert a great influence; this does not merely involve Pudong, this has a vital bearing on Shanghai's development and use of the base—Shanghai for developing the Yangtze River Delta and the Yangtze River Basin. We must lose no time in developing Pudong and we must unswervingly develop it until its completion."[3] On the initiative of Comrade Deng Xiaoping, the third generation Central Committee of

---

[1]Exposition on Pudong's Development and Opening-up, prepared by the Office for Collection of Historical Materials of Pudong's Development and Opening-up, p. 17.

[2]*Outlook Weekly*, 1996(17), p. 4.

[3]*Selected Works of Deng Xiaoping* (VOL. 3), People's Publishing House, 1993, p. 366.

the Communist Party of China with Comrade Jiang Zemin as the core made the strategic decision to develop Pudong of Shanghai.

Pudong's development and opening up was a banner signifying China's further reform and opening up as set down by our Party at the crucial historical juncture amidst international vicissitudes and domestic political disturbance in the late 1980s and the early 1990s. Based on the historical pioneering establishment and experimentation of the special economic zones, our Party chose Shanghai—a city with the largest economic scale and extensive international influence in China—as the window for further intensifying reforms and expanding the opening up, fully demonstrating that our Party's determination and confidence in unswervingly undertaking the socialist road with Chinese characteristics and resolutely adhering to the Party's basic line, clearly answering the question about what course to follow for China, creating the conditions for breaking the sanctions and blockade imposed by Western countries.

(II) Functioning as flagship

Three generations of the central leadership inspected Pudong and four National Congresses of the Communist Party of China mentioned Pudong's development, giving prominence to the special functions and roles of Pudong. The 14th National Congress of the Communist Party of China explicitly stated: "We shall take the development and opening-up of Pudong of Shanghai as our flagship to further open the cities along the banks of the Yangtze River to the outside world and as soon as possible turn Shanghai into one of international economic, financial and trade centers so as to fuel a new economic leap in the Yangtze River Delta and the whole Yangtze River Basin", which identified the objective and positioning of the national strategy for Pudong's development. The 15th National Congress of the Communist Party of China encouraged Pudong to continue forging ahead in institutional innovations, industrial upgrading, expansion of the opening up and other fields, and serving as a national model, radiator and driver. The 16th National Congress of the Communist Party of China further stressed that Pudong should spearhead in institutional innovations, expansion of the opening up and in other fields, and defined the developmental requirement that Pudong's development should advance with the times. From a new historical starting point, the 17th National Congress of the Communist Party of China further underscored that more attention should be given to the important role of Pudong in reform, opening up and self-independent innovation, and further pinpointed the direction for Pudong at a higher starting point.

Comrade Deng Xiaoping once stated: "The late development of Pudong is a bad thing but also a good thing. You can draw upon the experience from Guangdong Province to do better and make it more modernized, starting from a higher point."[4] Comrade Jiang Zemin stressed: "Pudong's development and opening-up was put

---

[4]Party History Research Office of Shanghai Municipal Party Committee of the Communist Party of China, *Deng Xiaoping and Shanghai's Reform and Opening Up*, Shanghai People's Publishing House, 1994, p. 318.

forward from the overall national economic developmental strategy, we must concentrate our efforts on carrying out Pudong's development well, continuously elevating Pudong's development and opening-up to new heights."[5] Comrade Hu Jintao required continued efforts to do a good job in Pudong's development and opening-up. He also thought it necessary to accelerate the institutional innovations, increase the outward-looking economic level, and achieve rapid development from a higher starting point."[6]

Facts prove that Pudong's function as a flagship has been embodied; with Pudong's development and opening up, Shanghai's economy has grown at a double-digit rate for 16 consecutive years, the look of the city has greatly changed, and the city has transformed from an industrial base to a multifunctional economic center. At present it is moving towards the ambitious goal of becoming an international economical, financial, trade and shipping center and a modern socialist international metropolis. Pudong's development and opening-up has stimulated a great leap forward for the economy in the Yangtze River Delta and the Yangtze River Basin, shaping an important pole of growth for the rapid development of China's economy.

(III) Serving as a window

The roles of Pudong as "window" and "stage" have been more and more prominent, and its functions as "model" and "driver" have been increasingly enhanced. Pudong's development as a window demonstrates the determination and capability of the people of the Communist Party of China for leading construction modernization, and displays the enormous energy resulting from combining the State will with the needs of advanced productive forces under the leadership of the Communist Party of China. Many foreign leaders who have visited Pudong have admired the great progress made in Pudong and have witnessed the changes in China through Pudong. Some people who had doubts about China's developmental path have also understood what socialism with Chinese characteristics is "Pudong's development and opening up has served as a hub in the transformation of China's reform and opening up from south to north, east to west and single point to complete area. It is not only the window and important mark for China's reform and opening up, but also the experimental field for China to intensify reforms and build a system of a socialist market economy. It is the forerunner of the adjustment of China's economic structure and construction modernization as well as a vivid model of successful development and opening up in the eastern coastal areas of China."[7]

The vivid practice of Pudong's reform and opening up proves the profound connotation of the times of Deng Xiaoping's Theory, the important thought of the

[5]*Jiefang Daily*, Speeches during the Inspection Tour in Shanghai, November 23, 1992.

[6]Exposition on Pudong's Development and Opening-up, prepared by the Office for Collection of Historical Materials of Pudong's Development and Opening-up, p. 26.

[7]Chen Gaohong, Zhou Suyuan, Li Youlin et al., Vivid Practice of Socialism with Chinese Characteristics—Inspirations from Pudong's Reform and Opening Up, *Qiushi*, 2008(18), p. 38.

Three Represents and the outlook on scientific development. It reflects the developmental requirements for combining the State will with the contemporary advanced productive forces. It embodies the strategic choice of socialist China for keeping in step with the times and gaining a firm foothold in the fierce international competition. It gives expression to the successful exploration made by China in following the socialist road with Chinese characteristics to make the country prosperous, its people well-off and make the nation revive. It shows the vibrancy of Shangahi—a Chinese megacity—in seizing great opportunities and overcoming various difficulties in order to thrive and develop. It also reflects the mental outlook of the people involved in Pudong's development and construction for taking up the national mission and blazing new trails in a pioneering spirit.

3 Factor Characteristics of a Market Economy

If we suppose that the initial conception of the establishment of special economic zones aims at proving that economic development can be achieved under the context of socialism, Pudong's development and opening up is one of the models proving that the market economy is also feasible in socialism after the South Inspection Speeches of Comrade Deng Xiaoping. Pudong's development and opening up is an important mark of the intensification of the reform of China's economic system. In 18 years, since Pudong's development and opening up, we have always firmly practiced the strategies that "development is the first priority for the Party to govern and rejuvenate the country" and "it is imperative for unswervingly pursuing Pudong's development." We have advanced along the direction guided by the outlook on scientific development and have not gotten lost. In that period, the market-oriented allocation of economic factors was achieved; domestic and foreign resources were effectively integrated; comprehensive economic strength significantly improved; the total output value soared from 6 billion yuan in 1990 to 275.1 billion yuan in 2007, an annual average growth rate of 18.2%; the total fiscal revenue skyrocketed by 77 times compared with the 1990s. The proportion of its economic aggregate in Shanghai's economic aggregate increased from 1/12 in 1990 to nearly 1/4 in 2007, with its economic aggregate equivalent to the economic scale of the whole of Shanghai in the early 1990s.

(I) Marketization of factors

The most outstanding contribution from Pudong's development lies in making breakthroughs through the market-oriented allocation of production factors and exploring the establishment of a relatively improved factor market system to intensify the reform from the marketization of general consumer goods to such production factors as capital, land, labor and technology. The establishment of these factor markets has greatly improved the efficiency of the utilization of massive potential resources (capital, land, technology, talents) and has enhanced the overall quality and the international competitiveness of the economy.

With the support of the Central Government, Pudong became the first to establish the Shanghai Stock Exchange, Futures Exchange, Diamond Exchange and other factor markets to gather more than 500 domestic and foreign financial institutions, preliminarily shape a relatively enhanced financial market system including banking, insurance, securities, futures, trust and funds, thus continuously developing the financial factor markets, promoting a close combination of capital and various production factors, greatly increasing the role of finance in economic integration and improvement, improving the efficiency of economic operations and emancipating the productive forces. In addition, the construction of a labor market, technology, assets and equity exchange markets has been carried out by establishing the Shanghai United Assets and Equity Exchange to offer an important platform for enabling the orderly flow of state-owned assets, promoting a connection among science, technology and capital, providing foreign capital and cross-border mergers and acquisitions with access channels, facilitating the market-oriented allocation of state-owned property rights resources so as to carry out and deepen the state-owned enterprise reform at the property rights level in a standardized, orderly fashion.

(II) Economic openness

Pudong's people have highly valued the opportunities and challenges presented by economic globalization and have fully leveraged both domestic and foreign markets, and domestic and foreign resources. Pudong's people have endeavored to do something while refraining from doing something else, energetically developing the outward-looking economy, introducing domestic advantageous resources amid development, gathering the quintessence of the world's economy during the opening up, implementing the industrial developmental policy for giving the first priority to finance and trade, high and new technology industries, vigorously cultivating and introducing industries and large corporations with international competitiveness. In 18 years, since Pudong's development and opening up, a cumulative 16,164 foreign-funded projects have been attracted from more than 100 countries and territories; contractual foreign investments and actual foreign investments amount to 40.7 billion USD and 23.9 billion USD, respectively; the rate of contribution from foreign enterprises to the economy of the New Area has exceeded 70%, and more than 10,000 enterprises from domestic provinces and municipalities have invested in Pudong.

Most of the more than 10,000 foreign enterprises introduced to Pudong enjoy an advanced international technical level of manufacturing. A total of 255 among the global top 500 companies have invested in 404 projects in Pudong, making Pudong dispense with the primary processing stage of the three-processing and one compensation—processing of materials supplied by foreign clients, processing according to buyer's samples, assembling of parts supplied by foreign clients and compensation trade—and directly develop the advanced manufacturing industry and high and new technology industry, transform the industrial structure from a dominance of the industrial economy to a dominance of the service economy. As a result, the added value of the tertiary industry has annually grown by 22.3% on average, higher than the annual average growth rate of the total output value—18.2%; as the core sector of the tertiary industry, finance accounts for near 1/3 of the added value of the tertiary industry; the commercial service industry dominated by headquarters economy and professional service has rapidly risen, accounting for 20% of the tertiary industry.

(III) Degree of the industrial chain connection

Four national-level developmental zones, the Lujiazui Finance and Trade Zone, the Waigaoqiao Bonded Area, the Jinqiao Export Processing Zone and the Zhangjiang Hi-tech Park, within the Pudong New Area have become the important function carriers for building Shanghai into an international economic, financial, trade and shipping center. In these four national-level developmental zones, a seamless connection in the industrial chain among enterprises has been achieved; components, parts and complete machine factories are relatively concentrated, while services concerning customs, taxation, banking and logistics are available at "zero distance". For example, the Lujiazui Finance and Trade Zone is home to many domestic and foreign financial institutions and has seen the preliminary formation of a relatively perfect financial market system covering banking, insurance, securities, funds and trust; the Waigaoqiao Bonded Area has continuously improved in its bonded logistics and port functions, where the operating revenue of logistics enterprises reached 205.3 billion yuan and the turnover of the bonded market was nearly 60 billion USD in 2007; as an important advanced manufacturing base in Shanghai, the Jinqiao Export Processing Zone delivered a total industrial output value worth 159.5 billion yuan in 2007; the Zhangjiang Hi-tech Park has brought together about 1000 enterprises, research and development institutions and specialized colleges of well-known higher education institutions, where industry-university-research integration is realized; the clustering effect of high and new technology industries, including the software, integrated circuits and biopharmaceutical industries has preliminarily taken shape, and a number of innovative enterprises with proprietary intellectual property rights and international competitiveness have stood out.

4 Evolution of Government Functions

The successful practice of Pudong's development and opening up is attributable to the wise leadership of the Central Government and to the generous support of people across the country. Such successful practice is a result of all-out efforts from the Shanghai Municipal Party Committee and the Shanghai Municipal Government. At the beginning of Pudong's development, the Shanghai Municipal Party

Committee and the Shanghai Municipal Government set up a special leading group for Pudong's development for studying and addressing major issues. At the stage of the most intensive development of Pudong, the leading group, bi-weekly, convened a joint meeting for addressing issues in a centralized way. Thanks to this great care and strong support, Pudong was provided with sufficient space and forces dedicated to development and construction from the beginning; an efficient and streamlined managerial framework has been built, and government functions are constantly transformed along with the intensification of development and opening up.

(I) Streamlining the government administration

The Shanghai Municipal Party Committee and the Shanghai Municipal Government adopted the new area, new things and new measures, actively encouraged Pudong to conduct institutional innovations, supported Pudong to act on its own, handle special matters with special methods so as to provide a strong guarantee for the first implementation and experimentation in Pudong. In Pudong, a new type of managerial system characterized by small governments and a large society has been explored, and government departments have been set up under the principle of putting the Party and the government in one working place, separating government administration from enterprise management, strengthening comprehensive departments, exercising a large system management; departments and personnel have decreased by 2/3 and 1/3, respectively; the functions of 4–5 departments under the traditional system have been integrated into one department, and the original coordination relationship among departments has been changed to a working relationship within departments, thus greatly reducing the difficulties in balancing and coordination, mitigating the friction among departments and enhancing the efficiency of management operations. Active experimentations have been carried out in performing one-door services, intensifying the reform of the administrative approval system, canceling administrative and institutional fees, stopping and suspending their collection. The government has been transformed from a control-oriented government to a service-oriented government. The number of items subject to administrative examination and approval has been reduced from 724 before the reform to the current 220. Nongovernmental organizations are constantly cultivated and developed.

(II) First developing plan

Pudong's people have adhered to the principle of high-standard, systematic planning and have broken away from the model of urban development based on the blind expansion of scale, and have creatively put forward the planning philosophy of "function division and multi-core group" to carry out urban formation and industrial planning according to functional positioning. With a focus on financial and trade development, scientific and technological innovation and other functions, four distinctive developmental zones with different functions, the Lujiazui Finance and Trade Zone, the Waigaoqiao Bonded Area, the Jinqiao Export Processing Zone and the Zhangjiang Hi-tech Park, were planned and established at the earliest.

Pudong International Airport was planned and built later, and it has become an important transport and logistics hub. The main venue for the 2010 Shanghai World Expo was planned and arranged in the Sanlin Area, and it has become an important area for exhibitions and the development of tourism in Pudong. Under this overall plan, the overall urban developmental layout of "one axis" (Shanghai urban developmental axis from Shanghai Hongqiao Airport to Pudong International Airport), three belts (the developmental belt along the Huangpu River, the central developmental belt, the riverside and seaside developmental belt) and six zones [six function zones: Lujiazui, Zhangjiang, Jinqiao, Waigaoqiao, Sanlin World Expo, Chuansha (Airport)] have basically taken shape in Pudong. In the design of the urban plan, the international planning bidding has been conducted for major areas, major projects and landmark projects; for example, the planning for small Lujiazui was based on the first international bidding concerning urban planning in China, which brought together a galaxy of world-class planning masters and outstanding representatives.[8]

(III) Fostering a business-friendly environment for the promotion of business

Pudong first gave birth to the way of thinking of moving from "resource-based business promotion" to "environment-based business promotion", developing "innovation highland" by "talent highland". Besides, it is dedicated to promoting enterprise development and talent agglomeration by a good environment and services. Ecological consciousness is highlighted, and efforts are being made to avoid city diseases, common in large cities, such as space congestion and severe environmental pollution. The industries with low energy consumption and low pollution are favored. The newly introduced projects are subject to a one-vote veto in terms of environmental protection, and the economy is, by no means, developed at the expense of the environment. The total amount of green space in Pudong is 25 times what it was at the beginning of the development, and the area of per-capita public green space is 45 times what it was at the beginning of the development. Pudong has been awarded various titles, including the "National Garden City Area" and the "National Model City Area for Environmental Protection". The Zhangjiabang River Control and Improvement Project, the Solid Waste Recycling Project have been awarded the China Habitat Environment Example Prize and the UN Award for Best Practices to Improve the Living Environment. In response to the new situation and new issues in the economic field, the first judicial tribunal for intellectual property rights at the grass-roots court and the first financial arbitration court were established nationwide. The scientific and technological investment and financing system is continuously improved. The Government Venture Capital Guidance Fund worth 2 billion yuan has been launched to address capital bottlenecks for small and medium-sized innovative enterprises. Incubator and public service platforms are being earnestly built to cut down innovation costs for enterprises and to promote the

[8]Zhao Qizheng, Pudong's Logic—Pudong's Development and Economic Globalization, Shanghai Joint Publishing House, 2007, p. 39.

agglomeration and integration of innovative resources. Actions are being taken to build a talent highland, and create a good environment for household registration, housing and children's education, actively explore a contribution-based mechanism for production factors, implement a talent internationalization strategy, strengthen the development of an entrepreneurial group of returned students, cultivate innovation teams and leading personnel to make Pudong become the broad stage for tapping the potential of domestic and foreign talents.

5 The Integration and Harmony of Social Development

Promoting coordinated social development while maintaining rapid economic development is an issue shared by economic developmental zones and also an important benchmark for measuring the development and construction achievements. In Pudong, coordinated economic and social development is pursued and a sustainable developmental pattern under which production has been developed, people are well-off and ecology is good has preliminarily taken shape.

(I) Coordination of urban and rural development

Most of the Pudong Area was a rural area and the foundation for social undertaking was weak before Pudong's development. In order to address accelerated urbanization and inflow of a large population since after the development and opening up, the Shanghai Municipal Party Committee and the Shanghai Municipal Government have been actively supporting social undertaking and cultural development in Pudong while pushing forward the rapid development of Pudong's economy by newly building and expanding a number of educational, medical, health, cultural and sports facilities, vigorously pressing ahead with the reform of a social undertaking management system, integrating urban and rural basic education, medical treatment and health, social security management systems, and separating social undertaking regulations from their management, as well as boosting an intensive, balanced development of social undertakings.

Pudong's development is a process of rapid urbanization. Properly dealing with the relations between the developmental zone and the town, between the development construction and the protection of farmers' interests has a vital bearing on the success of Pudong's development. The "Train Project" was launched at the early stage of Pudong's development and opening up so that the national-level developmental zone served as the "locomotive" for driving the development of suburban towns. The strategy of "flying wing to wing, fostering linkage development" was implemented at the stage of the relatively mature development of the developmental zone, and the linkage between districts and towns was built and advantages were complemented with each other to quicken the economic development of suburbs and the construction of small towns. In 2005, emphasis was placed on functions by establishing six function zones in Pudong, and the boundary between urban and rural areas was broken at the level of the managerial system so as to promote urban and rural integrated development. Meanwhile, in the process of Pudong's development and opening up, farmers' interests were always protected, and the resettlement measure of "two-guarantee one-compensation" plus "one-service" was first explored, a certain economic compensation was provided to farmers whose land was requisitioned, and all of these farmers were incorporated into the social security system so as to ensure endowment insurance and medical insurance for them; moreover, the employment service system was extended to rural areas to provide farmers with employment training services, and employment issues concerning these farmers were addressed through market mechanisms.

(II) Extensibility of co-construction and sharing

The success of Pudong's development and opening-up is attributable to extensively recruiting the talents, pooling the wisdom of the people, and making people support and participate in the developmental construction. Such success is embodied in people sharing in the development, opening-up and construction achievements. With the rapid economic and social development in Pudong, the people's living standard has constantly improved. Per-capita disposable income of urban and rural residents in Pudong reached 24,273 yuan and 12,246 yuan respectively in 2007, up 14.9 times and 8.2 times compared with 1990. The per-capita housing area of urban and rural residents was 23 m^2 in 2007, being nearly two times what it was in 1990.

Pudong is no longer a cultural desert. There are diverse cultural forms including reading salons, communicative lectures, advanced studies, music appreciation, and various characteristic activities including the day of the opening of the patriotism education base to the public for free, the Oriental Citizen Music Concert, the Pudong Oriental Forum, Citizen School Training, 100 artistic performances and 1000 movies in communities, attracting more and more citizens. Every year people enter bookstores and libraries for more than six million person-times, visit memorial halls and museums for more than 100 person-times, and attend lectures held by experts and scholars near home for more than 0.2 million person-times; nearly 4000 movies are shown in village committees and neighborhood committees. More than 3000 mass cultural teams are active in streets, towns and communities. Cultural performances take place in the squares of communities (residential quarters) every day. Nearly 100 mass artistic performances at different levels are available every month. People take part in activities for cultural and ideological progress for more than one million person-times every year. The days during which "merely one bed in Puxi is eagerly coveted by people, while even one room in Pudong cannot allure people" have gone. Pudong has become the paradise for Chinese and foreign people to start business and the homeland for citizens to live and work in.[9]

[9]Li Youlin, Pudong: 18 Years Old, Radiant, *Pudong Development,* 2008(4), p. 18.

(III) Inclusiveness of the humanistic spirit

The Pudong New Area consists of all or part of the areas of the original three districts and two counties in Shanghai. Pudong has become an important population inflow area and the area for gathering domestic and foreign talents, migrant workers in Shanghai in only 18 years. There is a permanent resident population of more than 3 million from various places at home and abroad, from urban and suburban areas; although they have different cultural backgrounds, different religious faiths and different language foundations, all of them are attracted by the undertaking of Pudong's development and opening up, and influenced by the vitality of Pudong's development and opening up, and different groups accommodate with each other in communication and coexist in harmony. Pudong is not only the paradise where Chinese and foreign people start business, but also the homeland where citizens live and work. Pudong has nearly 30,000 domestic and foreign enterprises, more than 30,000 foreigners, 48 foreign-related residential quarters, nearly 0.5 million white-collar workers, more than 1 million migrant workers. Chinese and foreign people cooperate and coexist, recognize each other's values to foster a regional culture with Pudong's characteristics. Domestic and foreign enterprises engage in win-win cooperation for interactive development to promote a modern industrial civilization. From cultural recognition to social value recognition, from enterprise development to park and industrial development, the philosophies "get along harmoniously with and treat each other sincerely", "encourage success, tolerate failure", "choose Pudong, choose success" are not only incorporated into the industrial developmental process, but also internalized as the mental quality and life attitude of Pudong's people.[10]

6 Innovation-Driven Development of First-Class Party Building

The course of Pudong's development and opening up is rooted in the general background of China's reform and opening up. It not only possesses the times characteristics of China's social transformational period, but it is also concentrated in 18 years of rapid development. Pudong's development and opening up are an iconic event in all-round reform and opening up in China in a specific historical period and a modernization undertaking which demonstrates the governing capacity of our Party and tests the construction of grass-roots organizations of our Party. The practice of Pudong's development proves that as reform and opening up deepen further, it is more necessary for strengthening the building of our Party, constantly enhancing the governing capacity of our Party, maintaining and developing the advancement of our Party.

[10] Li Youlin, Pudong: 18 Years Old, Radiant, *Pudong Development,* 2008(4), p. 19.

(I) First-class Party building promotes first-rate development

In 18 years, since Pudong's development and opening up, besides the traditional old residential quarters, a new type of community, including new commercial residential quarters, foreign-related international communities, rural urbanized communities, rural and urban mixed communities, non-native agglomeration areas and new economic organizations and new non-governmental organizations massively emerged. Communities are diverse in form; various groups gather together, and new types of organizations spring up. At its inception in 1993, the Party's Working Committee of the Pudong New Area clearly put forward the guiding thought that "first-class Party building promotes first-rate development"[11] We insist on enhancing the Party building by focusing on development, which then can promote development. The "Three-cohesion", "three-service" and "three-coverage" Party building innovative way of thinking gradually takes shape in practice. With the aim of cohering the Party members, the masses and society, based on that superior organizations of the Party serve grass-roots organizations, grass-roots organizations of the Party serve the Party members, the Party's organizations at various levels and the Party members serve the masses, and with a guarantee through coverage provided by organizations, work and systems, the Party's work covers every corner of the developmental construction. The practice that the "Party branch is built upstairs" was first adopted.[12] As the Party building is effectively carried out through Party building innovations and Party member "sunshine stations" in the developmental zone, the cohesive force, fighting capacity and influence of Party organizations are consolidated and strengthened.

(II) Incorrupt government also represents an investment environment

Developmental construction and the construction of a clean government system are concurrently conducted in the Pudong New Area, and it is stressed that incorrupt government also represents an investment environment.[13] Three "high-tension lines"—do not, for some improper purposes, break a rule, write a brief informal note, give a previous notice to relevant departments with respect to land prices, housing prices, project positioning, preferential policies; they do not seek private gain through power in land requisition, removal and relocation, they do not abuse power to seek unjustified interests for relatives and friends; they do not abuse power to seek benefits in project contract awarding—are erected. Two "firewalls"—no person in charge of a development company is permitted to decide on a company's borrowing and lending without authorization, provide fund guarantee for others in the name of the company, which is subject to approval from the company's board

---

[11]Zhao Qizheng, Pudong's Logic—Pudong's Development and Economic Globalization, Shanghai Joint Publishing House, 2007, p. 234.

[12]Li Youlin, Thinking of Party Building in Communities during the Transformation Period—Take the Pudong New Area as an Example, *Pudong Forum*, 2008(6), p. 30.

[13]Zhao Qizheng, Pudong's Logic—Pudong's Development and Economic Globalization, Shanghai Joint Publishing House, 2007, p. 235.

of directors and board of supervisors—are set up. A branch of discipline inspection is established. An accountability system, a complaint system, an evaluation system and an electronic supervision system are developed. The citizen hearing systems, major decision announcement systems are implemented, and online district head working meetings, citizen administrative discussion meetings are put into practice so as to build a public platform for administering affairs for the people and soliciting opinions from the people. Cadre work-style education is strengthened and the Pudong spirit mainly characterized by the awareness of striving for the best, the aspiration for making achievements and establishing undertakings, the realm for working wholeheartedly, the sentiment for honesty and self-discipline and being broad-minded are earnestly carried forward.

FSC
www.fsc.org
MIX
Papier | Fördert
gute Waldnutzung
FSC® C083411

Kolibri 360 GmbH
Ferdinand-Jühlke-Straße 7
99095 Erfurt, Deutschland
produktsicherheit@kolibri360.de